FORD AND CANADA

100 YEARS TOGETHER

JAMES C. MAYS

MONTREAL

National Library of Canada Cataloguing in Publication

Mays, James, 1953-

Ford and Canada : 100 Years Together

Issued also in French under title: Ford et le Canada.

ISBN 0-9733812-0-5

1. Ford Motor Company of Canada--History. 2. Automobile industry and trade--Canada--History. I. Title.

HD9710.C24F67 2003   338.7'6292'0971   C2003-904866-7

Cover design and layout by Harold Schnell

Printed by Xerox Canada Limited
Oakville, Ontario, Canada

First Edition
First printing August 2003

PROLOGUE

It began in 1904. Although it was barely one year old, Ford's first step outside the United States was into Canada, when Henry Ford and Gordon McGregor created the Ford Motor Company of Canada, Limited in Windsor, Ontario – a venture that established the Canadian automobile industry, as we know it today.

As this historical book recounts, Henry Ford and Gordon McGregor wrote the rulebook for Canadian entrepreneurs in the last century. With such a rich legacy, in many ways we will be rewriting some important chapters to guide entrepreneurs for the next 100 years.

Today, Ford is a proud partner in Canadian industry, with a national headquarters, six regional offices, three vehicle assembly plants, three engine manufacturing plants and two engine component plants, two parts distribution centres, and Canadian affiliates including Ford Credit, Volvo, Aston Martin, Jaguar, Land Rover and Hertz. Ford of Canada employs more than 16,000 people, while an additional 21,000 are employed in 500 Ford and Ford-Lincoln dealerships across Canada.

From our roots in a Windsor wagon factory, Ford of Canada has grown to be the country's fourth largest privately held company, with revenues for Canadian operations of more than $23 billion. Since 1990, Ford has invested nearly $9.5 billion in its Canadian operations, and we are growing our Canadian purchasing from $4.5 billion last year to $7 billion by mid-decade. We are a company whose legacy of investments and jobs has helped provide five generations of Canadians with one of the highest standards of living in the world.

The story of Ford is one of building, and continuous improvement. Together with all of our partners – our employees, dealers, unions, suppliers and customers – Ford has reached a point that few companies ever achieve. As we enter our 100th year in business in Canada, the roots of our past form a solid foundation to move forward into our future.

Alain Batty
President and CEO
Ford Motor Company of Canada, Limited

Through her dealings as business manager of the home, the modern woman brings sound commercial sense to bear on her judgment of a Ford closed car.

She knows that its low first cost, its small upkeep and operation costs, and its long-sustained usefulness make it a genuine economy. She is aware that the ease with which she can get expert attention for it anywhere and at any time is an asset of great dollar-and-cents value to her.

And she is delighted to find this value in a car that she drives so easily, and whose outward style and inward comfort she so whole-heartedly approves.

| TUDOR SEDAN, $590 | FORDOR SEDAN, $685 | COUPE, $525 | (All prices f. o. b. Detroit) |

CLOSED CARS

1924 Ford Closed Cars Pictorial Review

FOREWORD

In this wonderful historic book you will see how Ford in its early years transformed Canada and helped to pioneer and unite this vast country of ours. By establishing branches across Canada, Ford helped to put Canada on wheels which in turn pushed road construction from coast to coast.

As resources became available the company expanded globally to establish plants in South Africa, Australia, India, Malaya, Singapore, New Zealand and Rhodesia, and by 1947 accounted for 40 percent of the shipments from Ford in Windsor. Today, because of economic or political reasons only Australia and New Zealand are still in operation from the original group.

Reflecting on the events recorded over the years we must give praise to the insight of the company for successfully surviving many difficult obstacles such as the multitude of competitive nameplates fighting for a small market in the first few years, the affect of wartime production and shortages, the depression of the '30s, the influx of imported vehicles, and currency fluctuations in the last several years. The company, however, has taken advantage of every opportunity to enhance its value and growth. An excellent example was the Auto Trade Pact in 1965 which changed the direction of the auto industry in Canada. Ford quickly invested in facilities and products to successfully service the total North American market, with 90 percent of Ford's production now exported to the United States.

Over a span of 100 years this book chronicles major events in Canada and at Ford and emphasizes the appointment and importance of a strong dealer organization to provide quality sales and service to every community across Canada.

This book shows how Canada has prospered and changed during 100 years of glorious and exciting history and in the last 35 years as a key player in the total North American market. We must thank the dedicated employees, suppliers and dealers who have contributed to this rich heritage and established the platform for another vibrant century.

Kenneth W. Harrigan O.C.
Past President and CEO
Ford Motor Company Canada, Limited

 v

1946 FORD with many advancements now in production!

There's a *Ford* in your future!

Here is the most beautiful Ford car ever built—with more improvements than many pre-war yearly models ... Under the broad hood there's a V-8 engine with longer life—plus improved economy in oil and gasoline ... Interiors give you room to relax in luxury ...

Springs are of a new type and assure a level ride. The hydraulic brakes have been newly-designed—for quick, smooth, quiet stops ... Watch for announcements by your nearest Ford dealer. FORD MOTOR COMPANY OF CANADA, LIMITED

1946 Ford of Canada Poster

  vi

Introduction

When James first approached me with the proposal to write a book on Ford of Canada's Centennial I was pleased to give him as much assistance as possible, as I had always believed that Ford of Canada has a story that needs to be told. James' love of history and his dedication to researching all his subjects thoroughly is apparent in all of his book & article credits – he delights in the detail, the little-known facts, and his refreshing style of writing appeals to readers at every level.

When I started here in 1986 as assistant to the first Archivist of Ford of Canada, Herman Smith, I became intrigued by the early origins of this company started by an unassuming entrepreneur named Gordon McGregor, who always seemed to be in the background as the company flourished (he never wished to become President) and died an untimely death in 1922. It has been my pleasure & privilege for the past seventeen years to ensure that the fascinating history of Ford of Canada be preserved.

At the turn of the century Canada was a young country struggling to forge its own identity, and as the progress of the country is documented in this book, so too is the progress of Ford of Canada. This progress consisted of the small steps made – the fact that in 1908 our first Canadian coin was struck in Ottawa – to the huge changes, such as the signing of the Auto Pact in January 1965. Through all these changes, the constant theme is one of steady growth and success for both the Company and Canada. The title "Ford and Canada: 100 Years Together" reflects the bond that has always existed.

To James, I extend my sincere thanks for his dedication to a subject we both love, and to all the people then & now who are Ford of Canada I extend my heartfelt congratulations on one hundred years of making history.

Sandra Notarianni
Archivist, Ford of Canada

Ford of Canada Employees in 1914

DEDICATION

*T*o the men and women of the Ford Motor
    Company of Canada Limited, automotive
pioneers – past, present and future.

2004 Canadian Built Ford Freestar

 X

FORD AND CANADA

~ ~ ~ ~ ~

100 YEARS TOGETHER

Model C

August 17, 1904. Henry Ford and Gordon McGregor ink a deal that makes McGregor's Walkerville Wagon Works a producer of automobiles in Canada and throughout the British Empire. The new company has 17 employees and the first year's payroll will be $12,000. It is a bold move, there were only 182 horseless carriages in Ontario at the end of 1903. Ford will turn out 20 to 25 cars by year's end and will build a total of 117 cars in its first twelve months.

August 29, 1904. The stockholders of The Ford Motor Company of Canada, Limited holds its first meeting. Gordon McGregor is voted in as Secretary to the board and General Manager of the company.

~ ~ ~ ~ ~

September 29, 1904. The Earl of Grey is named the new Governor-General of Canada. He will give his name to the most coveted prize in football—the Grey Cup.

~ ~ ~ ~ ~

November 7, 1904. Edmonton, in the Northwest Territories is granted city status. The city will become Alberta's capital within a year. European settlement dates back to 1795 when it was a Hudson Bay post.

~ ~ ~ ~ ~

February 20, 1905. The first sale of Canadian-built Fords is recorded. Two Model C's and a Model B are shipped by express, the new owner wants it in a hurry. The purchaser is the Canada Cycle and Motor Company in Toronto who will pay the invoice of $3,545.

~ ~ ~ ~ ~

June 4, 1905. Daily train service from Montreal to Vancouver begins. Now, Fords can get to eager western owners much more quickly.

~ ~ ~ ~ ~

September 1, 1905. Alberta and Saskatchewan join Confederation as the eighth and ninth provinces.

November 8, 1905. A single Ford is shipped to New Zealand. It is the second of many Universal Cars to be built in Canada and shipped abroad.

~~~~~

December 31, 1905. Sales for the calendar year are $110,114. The workers have turned out 114 Model C units and seven of the Model B.

~~~~~

July 6, 1906. Citizens in Prince Edward Island vote for a dry province. One can't drink but one can still drive, cars won't be banned, yet.

~~~~~

July 11, 1906. The Lord's Day Act is official. Sunday is a day of rest. It is an acceptable activity to stroll through parks on Sunday afternoons and look at the latest beautiful automobiles on display by proud owners.

~~~~~

August 2, 1906. The first Canadian-made Fords are loaded onto a ship for export to the Commonwealth of Australia. They are all Model K.

~~~~~

December 31, 1906. Ford has built 101 automobiles this year of which 76 were exported and 25 were sold here at home.

~~~~~

July 1907. A Branch is opened in Toronto. Assembly will be added in 1916, during the war, to solve a box car shortage and end a shipping nightmare.

Augus 29, 1907. The new, unfinished bridge over the St. Lawrence River in Quebec City collapses, killing more than 80 workers.

~~~~~

December 31, 1907. Despite the business panic which has forced other companies into bankruptcy, Ford has built 327 automobiles. 236 are sold here at home and 91 are exported. The Model N is the most popular weighing at 1,050 pounds, costing only $500 and capable of hitting speeds of 40 miles an hour.

~~~~~

January 2, 1908. The first coin is struck at the Royal Mint in Ottawa. No longer will pocket change be shipped from Britain.

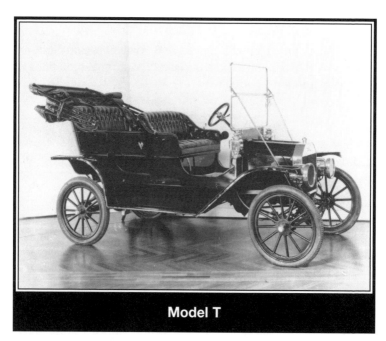

Model T

March 26, 1908. Members of the legislature in Charlottetown vote unanimously to ban all automobiles from Prince Edward Island.

~ ~ ~ ~ ~

October 1908. The first Model T rolls out the doors in Walkerville. It is the car that will put the nation on wheels.

~ ~ ~ ~ ~

January 11, 1909. Officials from Britain, Canada and the United States sign a treaty to preserve Niagara Falls.

~ ~ ~ ~ ~

September 1909. Ford of Canada opens an entirely Canadian-owned subsidiary in Australia. This is a brilliant move because more than half of the sales in Canada are between May and September, so production will roll right along, serving the needs of folks Down Under when their spring arrives in September.

~ ~ ~ ~ ~

October 1909. The Winnipeg branch of the Ford Motor Company is established. It is another bold move, there are only 34 motor cars in the entire province. The new territory consists of the three Prairie Provinces, with eight dealers in Alberta and 32 in Manitoba. The branch will sell 308 Fords during its first year of operation: 123 in Manitoba, 131 in Saskatchewan and 54 in Alberta.

~ ~ ~ ~ ~

April 20, 1910. Parliament votes to establish a Canadian Navy. It is to be small and put under "Imperial command" in the event of war.

August 1910. The frame building behind the old main factory in Walkerville is demolished to make room for a new, three-storey concrete building with 19,000 square feet of floor space. It will open in January of 1911.

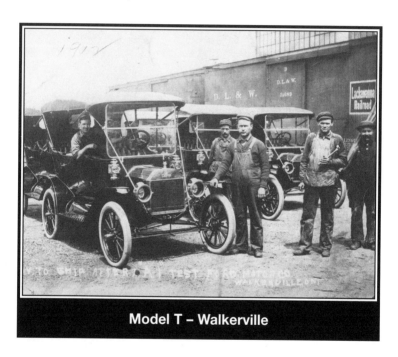

Model T – Walkerville

December 31, 1910. Ford has 118 employees on the payroll. The population of Canada is 7,206,643.

~ ~ ~ ~ ~

May 15, 1911. His Majesty's Royal Canadian Post Office purchases three Model T's to deliver the mail in Toronto. They will log 75,000 miles and still be running great in February of 1914.

Augo ust 1, 1911. Capital stock is increased from $125,000 to $1 million and the name of the company is changed to Ford Motor Company of Canada, Limited. A new four-storey building is started on Sandwich Street. It will be built out over the river to just inside the river bank for the power plant and cover 60,000 square feet.

~ ~ ~ ~ ~

September 1911. Located at 1233 Hornby Street in Vancouver, Ford opens a sales office to "distribute all Ford products west of the Canadian Rockies." There are eight employees.

~ ~ ~ ~ ~

September 21, 1911. Canadians vote "no" to free trade with the United States and sweep Laurier's Grits out of office. Sir Robert Borden and his Tories will form a new majority government.

~ ~ ~ ~ ~

October 1, 1911. There are two million people living in Quebec. Citizens boast 1,532 automobiles in *la belle province* of which 293 are Fords. Half a million live in Montreal which has slightly less than 1,000 automobiles, including 149 Fords.

~ ~ ~ ~ ~

November 3, 1911. The G.F. Stephens Company of Winnipeg writes that its Model T has already more than 7,000 miles on it and a repair bill of less than $5. "I have been able to work my territory with the Ford Model T in three weeks shorter time than formerly by train and at considerably less expense—from my experience I can heartily recommend it for either Country or City use." D.M. McIver.

December 31, 1911. Ford of Canada has 251 employees on payroll.

~~~~~

April 15, 1912. The *Titanic* sinks off the coast of Newfoundland.

~~~~~

June 1912 . Dick Bevean, a rancher in Creston, British Columbia buys three new Model T's. He will put 7,500 miles on his personal Ford at a total repair cost of $25. Not bad in a place where there are no roads yet.

~~~~~

August 8, 1912. Mr. B.L. Bishop of Greenwich, Nova Scotia purchases a new Ford. Even at 40 cents a gallon for gasoline he will find that his vehicle costs 1.5 cents a mile to operate.

~~~~~

December 9, 1912. The Bank of New Brunswick merges with the Bank of Nova Scotia. Folks won't be getting car loans from the new bank; that won't happen until 1957.

~~~~~

December 31, 1912 . Ford has 565 employees on payroll.

~~~~~

July 11, 1913 . To date, Saskatchewan has issued 1,730 licenses of which 595 were installed on Fords.

Ford Building – Saint John Branch

April 24, 1913. The legislature in Charlottetown votes to allow automobiles on the roads of Prince Edward Island on Mondays, Wednesdays and Thursdays. The ban on cars is modified because people fear that an auto-less island is hurting tourism.

~~~~~

May 20, 1913. Engines are no longer imported. The first Canadian-built Ford engines roll off the assembly lines.

~~~~~

Labour Day 1913. For the third year in a row, a Ford has won the Dunlop Trophy in a "spectacular twenty-five mile grind on a circular track" in Winnipeg.

October 1913. The new $1.5 million Hudson Bay Store has opened in Calgary. The deliveries will be made in six new Fords.

~ ~ ~ ~ ~

October 1913. "Doc" A.J. Gillis opens a Ford dealership in Dawson City, Yukon. When the first one is delivered aboard the steamer *Schwatka*, citizens gather along Front Street to cheer for the new owner and the Ford. 60 percent wood alcohol is the correct percentage to add to the rad in a Yukon winter.

~ ~ ~ ~ ~

November 1913. *The Ford Times* reports that 92 year old Eliza Smith of Wabush, Ontario is believed to be the oldest Ford owner in the world. She is reported to be "bright and happy and enjoys the best of health."

~ ~ ~ ~ ~

December 1913 . The City of Toronto purchases six new Fords, four for the Works Department, one for the Fire Department and one for the city's architecture department. That brings to 28 the number of Ford automobiles in daily use by the city.

~ ~ ~ ~ ~

December 1913. The Province of Alberta owns twenty-three motor cars. Eighteen of them are Fords.

~ ~ ~ ~ ~

December 1913. Freight rates for Fords from Windsor to are: Calgary $75; Hamilton $15; Montreal $25; Saskatoon $65; Saint John $32.50; Toronto $15; Vancouver $75 and Winnipeg $40.

December 13, 1913. The Chief of Police in Saskatoon writes to say that he has already put more than 3,000 miles on his Ford and has paid out nothing for repairs.

~~~~~

December 31, 1913. Ford has 931 employees on payroll.

~~~~~

January 1914. A new Ford Branch is established in Saint John, New Brunswick. Served by the Inter-Colonial Railway, it will deliver cars to Prince Edward Island where the ban on automobiles was recently partially lifted.

Ford Building – Toronto Branch

February 1914. The Royal North-West Mounted Police are authorized to spend $30,000 to purchase automobiles. They will buy Fords and McLaughlins.

~ ~ ~ ~ ~

March 14, 1914. Ford announces a new assembly and service plant to be built in Toronto at the corner of Christie and Dupont Streets. The five-storey building will house a large show-room and a garage with more than 12,000 square foot of space.

~ ~ ~ ~ ~

March 1914. The Ford plant covers sixty acres and has its own post office, Ford, Ontario.

~ ~ ~ ~ ~

May 29, 1914. *The Empress of Ireland* sinks near Quebec City. It is still the largest maritime tragedy in Canadian history.

~ ~ ~ ~ ~

August 4, 1914. Canada is at war, standing by Britain's side. The Royal Canadian Army has 3,110 regular soldiers. Within a few days more than 100,000 men will volunteer. They will be paid $1 a day.

~ ~ ~ ~ ~

August 4, 1914. The Province of British Columbia spends more than $1 million for two submarines to protect its consider-able coastline.

~ ~ ~ ~ ~

September 9, 1914. The Manitoba license list has 5,627 entries of which 2,057 are Fords.

September 1914. A farmer near Woodstock, Ontario is making a mint selling homemade ice cream to the neighbours at $1 a pound. "It would be impossible to do this without my Ford…it has turned out to be one of the most useful things on the farm."

~~~~~

December 31, 1914. Ford has 1,405 employees on payroll.

~~~~~

January 4, 1915. The first Canadian troops arrive in France.

~~~~~

January 11, 1915. E.A. Baldwin, the flour and feed mill dealer in Stanstead, Quebec writes "I am 61 years old have run the Model T without accident for four years and consider it good for as long as I shall want a car, if (I) should change it would be for another Ford."

~~~~~

January 20, 1915. The newly built American Hospital in Paris can handle up to 900 wounded soldiers. It uses 100 motorized ambulance trucks. There are Daimlers and a Dion-Bouton but there are more Fords than any other kind.

~~~~~

February 22, 1915. It is the grand opening for the Ford Branch building in Toronto. It cost $325,000. The week-long open house includes entertainment and a motion picture show produced by Ford's moving picture department.

Ford Ambulance

April 1, 1915. The Hanson Garage Company Limited opens its doors in Cranbrook, British Columbia. Ford is the product of choice at Hanson's.

~ ~ ~ ~ ~

April 16, 1915. Employees of the Ford Motor Company of Canada, Limited become the highest paid auto workers in the British Empire. They will earn 50 cents an hour or $4 a day. A worker will work only eight hours a day now, or 48 hours in a week. This affects the 2,400 employees in Ford, Ontario and its nine branches located in principal cities throughout the Dominion. The company can afford it; it is shipping 160 cars a day from the factory.

April 22, 1915. The Battle of Ypres begins today. 6,000 Canadians will die in the seven-day conflict. It is during this battle that Dr. John McCrea will pen the immortal words to the poem *In Flanders Fields*.

~ ~ ~ ~ ~

April 25, 1915. Watkin Motors Limited is ready to serve folks' needs up and down the Okanagan Valley from its sparkling new Ford dealership in Vernon, British Columbia.

~ ~ ~ ~ ~

August 1915. K. Matchett of Creemore, Ontario writes to Ford to say, "I have driven my Ford car 10,000 miles in all kinds of weather and road conditions without any trouble and with a total repair expense of $1.21."

~ ~ ~ ~ ~

September 21, 1915. Fairgoers to the Provincial Exhibition in Fredericton, New Brunswick are treated to a parade of more than 100 Fords on Ford Day. By arrangement with the city fathers, street sprinklers worked overnight so that "the procession drove through practically all the streets of the city without being inconvenienced by dust."

~ ~ ~ ~ ~

November 1, 1915. Ford leads all other carmakers in sales by four to one. Of the 22,070 automobiles sold in the past twelve months, 17,570 were Fords. Montreal has 3,917 automobiles, Toronto lists 8,815 registered cars, Victoria has 2,363 and Regina a total of 1,123 automobiles.

November 1915 . Under the title "Your true Canadian is a pioneer: our pioneer is a precedent-breaker. And your Ford is a true Canadian." *The Ford Times* reports that "patriotism burning with a passion of self-sacrifice swept the little town of Ford City, Ontario" as townspeople pledge $75,776.99 to the Canadian Patriotic fund and the Canadian and British Red Cross.

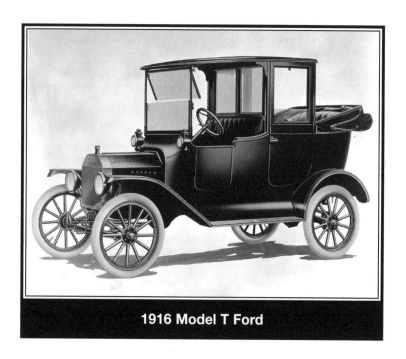

1916 Model T Ford

December 21, 1915. The Ford Motor Company of Canada, Limited is recapitalized to $10 million.

~~~~~

December 31, 1915. Ford has 1,867 employees on payroll.

January 1916. If all the Fords sold to date were parked bumper to bumper, they would form a line 1,730 miles long, stretching all the way from Toronto to Calgary.

~ ~ ~ ~ ~

February 1, 1916. Ford ships 214 automobiles today, the biggest output in the company's history.

~ ~ ~ ~ ~

February 4, 1916. The Parliament buildings in Ottawa burnt overnight. The Centre Block is completely gutted. It is widely believed that German spies are responsible. More than 1,000 solders are protecting the site.

~ ~ ~ ~ ~

March 1916. Ernest Bovaird of Hampton, New Brunswick writes to say that his Ford is "one of the best investments I ever made, in fact, it paid for itself within the first two months, in my livery business. Has run 6,000 miles—repairs eight cents."

~ ~ ~ ~ ~

May 9, 1916. Lieutenant-General Byng is named as the new head of the Canadian Corps.

~ ~ ~ ~ ~

June 1916. Folks who purchase a Ford should expect to pay an extra $44 for freight if they live in Canora, Fillmore, Kindersley, Moosomin, Saskatoon or Yorkton, Saskatchewan.

~ ~ ~ ~ ~

June 28, 1916. Ontario citizens vote to change the name of their city from Berlin to Kitchener, to show their loyalty to the Crown.

July 1916. From Grand Mere, Quebec comes this testimonial from J.A. Gagnon: "Cost of repairs during three years was about ten dollars. Proud to say my Ford has given me entire satisfaction."

~ ~ ~ ~ ~

July 1916. Since the beginning of the war Ford has added $1.75 million worth of buildings and hired more than 1,000 new employees.

~ ~ ~ ~ ~

July 1, 1916. Alberta becomes an officially dry province today. Alcohol is illegal except for medicinal purposes.

~ ~ ~ ~ ~

August 1916. Calgarians can trade in their horses for Fords at the country's newest Ford dealership, Central Garage, on 1st Street.

~ ~ ~ ~ ~

August 15, 1916. The Canadian Corps has 90,000 soldiers in three battalions. They are on the move to the Somme where they will join Australian and British troops.

~ ~ ~ ~ ~

September 15, 1916. The Allies have a new weapon in their arsenal; it is the first time in military history that a tank sees battle action.

~ ~ ~ ~ ~

November 8, 1916. The first Ford rolls out the doors of the new assembly plant in Toronto.

1916 Ford Touring Car

November 18, 1916. Assembly begins in Ford's newest plant. This one is in Montreal.

~~~~~

December 31, 1916. Ford has 2,879 employees on payroll. A new assembly plant has come on line in Winnipeg.

~~~~~

January 3, 1917. *The Toronto Globe* headline reads "Drop Passenger Trains to Move More Freight" as the war deepens and manufacturers' goods—including Ford's—can't get to market.

Ford Building – Winnipeg

February 7, 1917. The war continues to hamper shipment of goods. Local assembly of Fords begins in London, Ontario.

~~~~~

February 27, 1917. Women in Ontario can now vote in elections but they can not become Members of Parliament.

~~~~~

March 7, 1917. The first Ford made in the Maritimes is assembled at the new plant in Saint John, New Brunswick.

April 5, 1917. Women win the right to vote in British Columbia provincial elections.

~ ~ ~ ~ ~

April 9, 1917. Canadians lead the charge at Vimy Ridge. The slaughter will continue for six days. King George V will send a telegram to Ottawa praising Canada's victory over the German army.

~ ~ ~ ~ ~

May 1, 1917. The Federal Railways War Board, the Railway Commissions and the manufacturers' associations try to figure out how to deal with the critical shortage of boxcars. Short by some 200,000 cars, completed Fords and weapons of war can not get to the docks for shipment overseas.

~ ~ ~ ~ ~

June 2, 1917. Captain William "Billy" Bishop downs four German planes. The flying ace will receive the Victoria Cross for his bravery.

~ ~ ~ ~ ~

July 2, 1917. The Dent brothers, owners of the Ford dealership in Bothwell, Ontario, organize a "Monster Ford Picnic" for owners of the Universal Car. It is well attended and "a good time was had by all."

~ ~ ~ ~ ~

July 1917. The Canadian Pacific Railway purchases six new Fords. This adds to the seventeen in the fleet that the CPR ordered last spring. They will be used for "land seeking or inspection work" by officials. July 1, 1917 Canada turns fifty today but there are no celebrations because the nation is at war.

July 31, 1917. Bluenosers own 901 Fords and 287 McLaughlins, the second-best selling car in Nova Scotia. There are 3,907 Ford owners in Quebec and 782 McLaughlin owners, again the second best selling car in la belle province.

~~~~~

August 1, 1917. Mr. W. Warren opens a Ford dealership in picturesque Banff, Alberta.

~~~~~

August 8, 1917. Calgarians can get service for the Universal Car at Maclin Ford Sales.

~~~~~

September 1917. There are 36,218 Fords in Canada and 34,886 of all other makes combined. Ford dealers have sold 1,263 cars in Toronto this year and McLaughlin comes in second with 487 sales.

~~~~~

November 1917. In accordance with wartime rationing, beef consumption has dropped by almost 60 percent from this time a year ago.

~~~~~

November 1, 1917. The Hinton Family of Bathurst, New Brunswick opens the doors on their new Ford dealership. They will order vehicles from the new assembly plant in Saint John, New Brunswick. The Hintons will sell Fords for more than two decades.

November 26, 1917. The National Hockey League is signed into existence.

~~~~~

December 6, 1917. Halifax is rocked by an explosion as the *Mont Blanc* hits the *Imo* in the harbour and explodes. More than 1,600 citizens die in the deadly blast and more than 6,000 Haligonians are homeless, their houses flattened.

~~~~~

December 31, 1917. Ford has 3,382 employees on payroll. It is the country's biggest taxpayer, shelling out $1,782,094 to the Dominion Government. Imperial Oil Limited is a distant second, paying $734,046 to Ottawa.

1 1/2 Ton Delivery Truck

December 23, 1917. F.A. Penny of Mahone Bay, Nova Scotia calculates that the used, $400 Ford that he bought in June, has earned him $1,017.40 in profit.

~ ~ ~ ~ ~

January 1, 1918. There are a total of six trucks and 301 motor cars registered in Prince Edward Island.

~ ~ ~ ~ ~

February 1918. The new Ford One-Ton truck is introduced at $750 for the chassis. A national advertising campaign is launched to encourage farmers to switch from horse and mule power.

~ ~ ~ ~ ~

February 9, 1918. The federal government orders all businesses, stores and factories in Toronto to close for three days in order to conserve coal, a commodity desperately needed for the war.

~ ~ ~ ~ ~

March 4, 1918. Ottawa stations troops along the US border to stop would-be draft dodgers from escaping Ontario and fleeing into New York State.

~ ~ ~ ~ ~

April 1918. The government purchases 2,000 tractors and distributes them to farmers to help in farming operations since labour is in such short supply. Canadians are urged to eat fish, rabbit, beans and seafood instead of red meat. Ford employees pledge to eat one meatless meal a day.

~ ~ ~ ~ ~

May 8, 1918. Canadians own more than 200,000 automobiles, third behind the United States and the United Kingdom.

May 24, 1918. Women across the country now may vote in federal elections as long as they can prove they are British subjects and have reached 21 years of age.

Fordson Tractor

June 1918. Some kids in Edmonton are riding to school in an experimental, specially designed 15-passenger Ford truck. School officials in Calgary are looking into ordering the trucks for their children for the fall semester. They will be known as school buses.

~ ~ ~ ~ ~

June 6, 1918. As an emergency measure to avoid food rationing, Ford has sold 1,000 Fordson tractors to the Canada Food Board. 327 are shipped to Alberta, 349 to Saskatchewan, 200 to Ontario, nine to Quebec and six to New Brunswick.

June 17, 1918. The federal government warns that labour is so short that this year's crops will rot in the field. Ford offers to close its factories and send workers out to gather the harvest.

~~~~~

June 24, 1918. The nation's first airmail is delivered from Montreal to Toronto. The flight takes six hours.

~~~~~

October 1, 1918. Canadian troops have seized the Bourlon Wood, capturing more than 7,000 German soldiers.

~~~~~

October 22, 1918. The dreaded Spanish flu sweeps the nation. Vancouver reports 522 cases. Some 60,000 Canadians will die of the plague.

~~~~~

November 11, 1918. Germany, Turkey and Austria are defeated. At the eleventh hour of the eleventh day of the eleventh month, the war is officially over. Nearly 60,000 Canadian soldiers are buried in Europe, they gave their lives for King and Country. "If ye break faith with us who die, we shall not sleep, though poppies grow in Flanders fields."

~~~~~

December 31, 1918. There are 3,382 employees on Ford of Canada's payroll. All 9,901 Fords built this year can boast that they have 78 percent Canadian content.

~~~~~

January 29, 1919. The Ford shingle hangs over A. Horne & Company in Summerside, Prince Edward Island.

March 5, 1919. Homesick Canadian soldiers, stuck in Europe for nearly five years, riot for forty-eight hours. They want to go home. Troops are ordered to shoot at their comrades, 25 of the 800 are killed.

~~~~~

April 17, 1919. Women in New Brunswick may now vote in provincial elections.

~~~~~

June 6, 1919. Canadian National Railways is formed. The former private-sector railroads including the Inter-Colonial and Grand Trunk are nearly $50 million in debt. Taxpayers will pick up the tab.

~~~~~

July 31, 1919. The balance sheet shows a profit of $5,002,897.82 or $71.46 a share.December 31, 1919 With 2,730 employees on Ford's payroll, the average worker earns $6 an hour and that adds up to exactly $4,330,053 in wages.

~~~~~

December 31, 1919. With 2,730 employees on Ford's payroll, the average worker earns $6 an hour and that adds up to exactly $4,330,053 in wages.

~~~~~

January 16, 1920. Canada is a founding member of the League of Nations, signing in Geneva, Switzerland in hopes that civilized nations will never resort to another war.

February 1, 1920. The Royal Northwest Mounted Police become the Royal Canadian Mounted Police. The Mounties will drive Fords and they will always get their man.

~~~~~

February 26, 1920. By decree of Parliament, the Royal Canadian Air Force is established as a branch of His Majesty's Royal Canadian Armed Forces.

~~~~~

September 18, 1920. A total of 55,616 Ford automobiles has been sold in the just ended model year.

~~~~~

September 20, 1920. After experimenting for nearly a year, the world's first commercial radio station goes on the air in Montreal. XWA will change its call letters to CFCF standing for "Canada's First, Canada's Finest." The historic station will sign off forever in 1999.

~~~~~

December 31, 1920. Ford has 4,165 employees on payroll.

~~~~~

January 3, 1921. M.L. Wright & Son, Limited opens a Ford dealership in Perth, New Brunswick to serve the residents who live in the southern portion of Victoria County. No longer will they have to cross over to Fort Fairfield, Maine for service and parts. The Dominion Motor Car Company Limited in Saskatoon opens its doors for Ford, too.

March 26, 1921. *The Bluenose* is launched in Lunenburg, Nova Scotia. The America Cup winning schooner will be immortalized on the back of the dime.

~~~~~

May 12, 1921. Having recovered from the great fire of 1911, folks in Eganville, Ontario get a new Ford dealer as Boland and Watson hang up the blue oval. They will serve folks in Renfrew County.

~~~~~

September 26, 1921. The Director's reports shows that $343,700 worth of additions have been made to the Ford factory, primarily for machinery and equipment. Ford has also purchased the property it had been renting in Saint John, New Brunswick.

Gordon McGregor

December 31, 1921. There are 3,237 employees on Ford's payroll.

~~~~~

January 25, 1922. Dominion Motors Limited is Alberta's newest Ford dealership, located at 102nd Street and Jasper.

~~~~~

February 11, 1922. Doctors at the University of Toronto have discovered something they call insulin. The new drug will save the lives of millions of diabetics and earn Dr. Banting and Dr. Best the Nobel Prize in medicine.

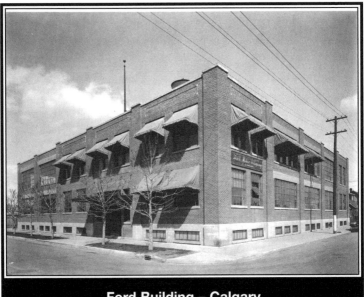

Ford Building – Calgary

March 11, 1922. Gordon McGregor, VP and General Manager of the company dies of complications sustained in an accident.

~~~~~~

March 16, 1922. The board of directors at Ford of Canada appoints Mrs. McGregor to a place on the board.

Ford Building – Regina

May 3, 1922. Women on Prince Edward Island can vote. Eight of Canada's nine provinces allow women to vote. In Quebec, women will wait until 1945.

~~~~~~

September 18, 1922. The company has sold 1,192 tractors for the year compared with 3,063 the previous year.

July 31, 1922. The fiscal report shows that a building for the Regina Ford Branch has been purchased for $66,727,57. The new Calgary operation has cost Ford $184,616.13

~~~~~

December 31, 1922. Ford has 3,427 employees on payroll.

~~~~~

January 16, 1923. K.C. Irving of Buctouche, New Brunswick opens a Ford dealership. K.C. Irving is Vice President and Mary E. Irving is secretary. The Irvings will be successful in other business ventures, too.

~~~~~

June 18, 1923. Folks in Kamloops, British Columbia can now have their Fords and Lincolns serviced at Dearborn Motors.

~~~~~

July 23, 1923. The Prime Minister of Newfoundland, Richard Squires, resigns in the midst of a scandal. He will be arrested for theft of public funds.

~~~~~

July 31, 1923. Ford has sold 70,328 passenger cars and 3,395 tractors to Canadians during 1922.

~~~~~

September 14, 1923. The value of the new Ford plants in Windsor and Toronto is determined to be $10 million.

October 22, 1923. Prime Minister Mackenzie King speaks at the Imperial Conference in London. He shocks the delegates when he tells the assembly that Canada wants its independence.

~ ~ ~ ~ ~

January 26, 1924. Canada gets a new flag. The Red Ensign, with the national coat of arms in the centre of a red field and the British flag in the upper left-hand corner will replace the familiar Union Jack. February 28, 1924 Lees and Alford hang out the Universal Car Sign so that folks in Oakville, Manitoba will know they have Fords to sell.

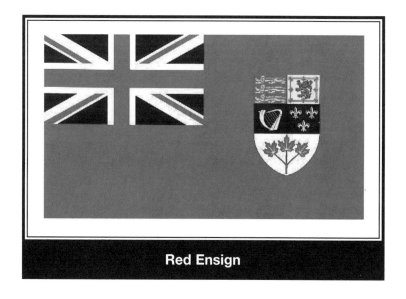

Red Ensign

March 15, 1924. At 819 Yates Street in Victoria, British Columbia, Ford owners can find sales and service at the country's newest dealership, National Motor Company, Limited.

September 26, 1924. The Ford Motor Company of Canada Limited has loaned $1,010,205.79 to its newly formed—as of December of 1923—and wholly owned subsidiary, The Ford Motor Company of South Africa Limited in Port Elizabeth. It will "serve the Union of South Africa, the Rhodesias and other African countries, primarily those within the Empire and using sterling as currency."

~~~~~

December 31, 1924. Ford has 4,988 employees on payroll. They earn $8,683,654 in wages.

~~~~~

February 23, 1925. Angry motorists arrive on the steps of Queen's Park in Toronto to protest the Ontario government's plan to impose a two-cent a gallon gasoline tax. The Premier brands the crowd as unpatriotic Canadians and tells them the tax won't be two cents, it will be three-cents on the Imperial gallon!

~~~~~

April 22, 1925. Assembly of marine engines begins in Ford City.

~~~~~

May 12, 1925. In Watrous, Saskatchewan it is J.E.D. McCord & Company that sells Fords. The town's other landmark—yet to be erected--will be the transmitting tower for CBK, sending the CBC signal throughout much of Saskatchewan and neighbouring Manitoba.

~~~~~

June 20, 1925. Stonehouse Motors Limited opens up shop in Vancouver. Folks in the neighbourhood can drop in to see and buy shiny new Fords.

September 8, 1925. Edward Flickenger, chief photographer for Ford of Canada climbs into a brand new 1926 Ford Model T in Halifax. After backing the rear wheels into the Atlantic Ocean, he and Dr. Perry Doolittle (one of the founders of the CAA and a major force behind the establishment of the Trans-Canada Highway) will drive the Tin Lizzie to Vancouver. It is a trip that will take until October 17. They will drive 4,794 miles, all of it through Canada. For 500 miles he will fit out the Model T with flanged railroad wheels and travel over train tracks because there is no road linking the country together. It will be the first complete cross-Canada trip by an automobile!

Model T Cross-Country Trip

September 22, 1925. 47 percent of Ford Canada's products are exported this year.

Decemeber 31, 1925. Shareholders have grown from 60 in 1904 to 3,021 in 1925. Now that the Russell company is gone, Ford is the only auto maker that is not totally foreign owned. Ford boasts 6,503 employees, 3,300 dealers and 8,754 authorized service garages across the nation's nine provinces.

~ ~ ~ ~ ~

December 31, 1925. Since 1911, a total of 360 cars and trucks and six tractors have been imported into the Dominion of Newfoundland.

~ ~ ~ ~ ~

February 1, 1926. The ink is drying on the paper. Now Ford owners in Red Deer, Alberta are served by Whyte Motors Limited.

~ ~ ~ ~ ~

April 15, 1926. The loan to The Ford Motor Company of South Africa Limited is paid in full.

~ ~ ~ ~ ~

June 29, 1926. The nation is in constitutional crisis as Mackenzie King's government collapses and the Governor-General refuses to dissolve Parliament for new elections. Lord Byng will order the Leader of the King's Loyal Opposition to form a new government but it will last only three days before being defeated in a vote of non-confidence.

~ ~ ~ ~ ~

November 26, 1926. Canada's first foreign diplomat is named. Vincent Massey will be the Ambassador to the United States.

Decdember 31, 1926. A total of 85 new cars and two tractors were shipped to the Dominion of Newfoundland during the calendar year.

~ ~ ~ ~ ~

January 7, 1927. Dingwall Motors Limited is the latest Ford dealer to open up shop. Folks in Kenora, Ontario are glad.

~ ~ ~ ~ ~

February 21, 1927. The Owl Service Station in North Sydney, Nova Scotia becomes an authorized Ford dealer. Hard times will cause it to will bow out on April 27, 1931.

~ ~ ~ ~ ~

March 2, 1927. The Privy Council in London settles a long-standing dispute between the Dominion of Newfoundland and Canada as to where the boundaries of Labrador are.

~ ~ ~ ~ ~

April 9, 1927. Ford of Canada now owns subsidiaries in India and Malaya.

~ ~ ~ ~ ~

July 1, 1927. The Canadian National Railways loans its telegraph lines to the federal government for a Canada-wide radio broadcast from 23 stations for Dominion Day. Folks tune in from Sydney, Nova Scotia to Victoria British Columbia on some 400,000 receivers to celebrate the Dominion's Diamond Jubilee. The patchwork CN Radio network will become the CBC in 1936.

December 12, 1927. Henry Ford steps down as the President of Ford of Canada. He is replaced by son Edsel.

~~~~~

December 27, 1927. There is still leftover Christmas turkey in the icebox to be eaten but there are papers to sign. Les Ventes Ford Brunelles in historic St. Eustache, Quebec is the company's newest Ford dealer.

Model A

December 31, 1927. A total of 39 cars and trucks and two Ford tractors were shipped to the Dominion of Newfoundland during the year.

~~~~~

Februrary 1, 1928. The first Model A engine is produced in Windsor. CA1 is the starting code.

~~~~~

February 19, 1928. Canadian athletes win hockey gold at the Winter Olympics in St. Moritz.

~~~~~

March 1928. While the Americans have had the Model A in production since December of last year, teething problems have delayed domestic introduction until now. It is marketed as "The Real Canadian Car."

~~~~~

April 24, 1928. The Supreme Court in Ottawa rules unanimously that women are not persons. The Privy Council will overturn that decision on October 18, 1929.

~~~~~

May 11, 1928. W. C. Campbell reports that $1,464,109.00 has been spent for machinery and equipment to produce the Model A cars and Model AA trucks.

~~~~~

August 19, 1928. The nation's farmers are begging for trucks to help bring in the huge harvests. Ford sources axles from Timkin, an outside supplier, and beats the competition to market. By year's end, Ford of Canada will have produced 25,859 trucks.

~~~~~

March 26, 1929. Edsel Ford becomes chairman of the board and Wallace R. Campbell becomes president of the company.

June 10, 1929. Ottawa decrees that the Arctic is to be mapped and given Canadian names. Foreign explorers will now have to apply for permits. This measure is designed to keep the Danes and Americans out of our back yard.

~ ~ ~ ~ ~

October 29, 1929. The stock markets collapse in Montreal and Toronto.

~ ~ ~ ~ ~

November 22, 1929. A tidal wave hits Newfoundland's Burin Peninsula, killing 27 people.

~ ~ ~ ~ ~

July 28, 1930. Voters turf out Mackenzie King and his Grits. Richard Bennett and his Tories will form the government. When the PM doesn't move quickly enough to alleviate suffering during the Dirty Thirties, disenchanted voters will remove the engines from their cars, hook them up to horses and call them 'Bennett buggies.'

~ ~ ~ ~ ~

November 2, 1930. An automobile tunnel now links Windsor, Ontario with Detroit, Michigan.

~ ~ ~ ~ ~

December 31, 1930. Newfoundlanders buy 179 Ford cars and trucks during the calendar year. That figure will drop to 115 in 1931.

~ ~ ~ ~ ~

February 27, 1931. The federal government bans the importation of goods from the USSR because it is a Communist country.

April 7, 1931. The collapse of the Australian dollar and restrictions on currency leaving that country leaves Ford of Canada carrying a debt of $939,186,53 owed to its parent in Ford City, Ontario.

~~~~~

June 18, 1931. The Dirty Thirties arrive with a vengeance. During the week, dust storms have dumped more than 6,000 tons of topsoil on the city of Winnipeg.

~~~~~

July 6, 1931. The economy is so bad in Saskatchewan that the Canadian Red Cross steps in to help the 150,000 citizens who are in need of heat, food and clothing.

V-8 Engine

December 31, 1930. Ford of Canada is in the black and will pay stockholders $1.20 a share plus an extra 30 cents.

~~~~~

March 9, 1931. Mills Motors hangs up the blue oval sign in Annapolis Royal, Nova Scotia.

~~~~~

December 31, 1931. The net loss for the year is $1.384,757.19 on sales of 38,890 vehicles.

~~~~~

January 28, 1932. Belliveau Motors Limited is open for business in Church Point, Nova Scotia. Folks will soon be able to buy the new V-8 Fords at reasonable prices.

~~~~~

February 11, 1932. The V-8 Fords are under production in Windsor. Ford will be the only V-8 producer in Canada for several decades.

~~~~~

March 5, 1932. Some 10,000 angry Newfoundlanders storm the House of Assembly in St. John's and ransack the building.

~~~~~

May 16, 1932. Civil servants in Ottawa take a 10 percent pay cut.

May 24, 1932. Prime Minister Bennett's dream of the creation of a national radio network becomes law. The Canadian Radio Broadcasting Commission will replace the ragtag network currently running on the CNR's telegraph lines.

~ ~ ~ ~ ~

August 1, 1932. A new political party is formed in Calgary. The Co-operative Commonwealth Federation will one day become the New Democratic Party.

~ ~ ~ ~ ~

October 8, 1932. By Order-in-Council, work camps will be set up to deal with the nation's destitute. One out of every four Canadians is desperately looking for a job, some 70,000 men are living on the streets. Those lucky enough to get into the work camps will earn $1 a day.

~ ~ ~ ~ ~

December 31, 1932. Ford's net loss for the year is $5,206,736.59 on output of 25,218 units, including those for export to overseas subsidiaries. The assembly plant in Montreal has been closed. A total of sixteen Ford cars and three Ford trucks were exported to the Dominion of Newfoundland this year.

~ ~ ~ ~ ~

November 28, 1933. The country is $100 million in debt; it is a black day for Newfoundlanders as the House of Assembly surrenders its self-governing Dominion status. Men with families earn six cents a day on public works programmes and walk as far as five miles to and from the job.

December 21, 1933. Ford will pay shareholders $1.00 a share. W.R. Campbell, president, wrote, "This disbursement, while not merited by earnings from the year's operations was nevertheless considered justified by the Company's strong surplus and cash position."

~ ~ ~ ~ ~

December 31, 1933. Net loss at Ford for the year is reduced to $1,174,991.73. Ford has $6,273,951.94 in the bank.

~ ~ ~ ~ ~

January 1, 1934. Ford of Canada, Limited has shipped 19 new Fords to Newfoundland in the past fourteen months. Only three have V-8 engines.

~ ~ ~ ~ ~

May 7, 1934. Officials at His Majesty's Canadian Post Office denounces the latest fad sweeping the continent—chain letters.

~ ~ ~ ~ ~

May 10, 1934. A violent dust storm sweeps the Prairie Provinces. Motorists are stranded on the roads and farms are buried knee-deep in dirt.

~ ~ ~ ~ ~

May 28, 1934. The Dionne quintuplets make international news as the five identical Geminis are born in Corbeil, Ontario.

~ ~ ~ ~ ~

July 3, 1934. The Bank of Canada is created by Parliament. The new central bank will set national fiscal policy.

December 31, 1934. The economy is improving, the factory in Windsor and all of its branches across Canada have been profitable for the first time since 1930. Ford closes out the year in the black, showing a net profit of $1,878,112.91 on the sales of 48,917 units.

Vancouver Assembly Plant

May 28, 1935. Ford pays a dividend of 50 cents a share. The company will sell 79,844 units this year, more than double the total in 1934.

~~~~~

June 28, 1935. The old age pension bill receives royal assent and becomes law.

July 1, 1935. Some 2,000 unemployed workers from British Columbia, Alberta and Saskatchewan have ridden the rails to Regina. They riot, leaving one RCMP officer dead and many civilians injured. Prime Minister Bennett refuses to meet with the men, branding them as Communists.

~~~~~

July 5, 1935. The Canadian Wheat Board comes into existence.

~~~~~

October 14, 1935. Mackenzie King and his Grits trounce Bennett and his Tories. King will lower the tariff on automobiles from the United States, prompting Studebaker, Packard, Huppmobile and Reo to halt Canadian assembly of its cars.

~~~~~

November 1935. The new 1936 Ford models go into production and that includes the new assembly operation in Vancouver, British Columbia. The West Coast operation will need a new factory by 1937.

~~~~~

January 9, 1936. Ford Motor Company of Canada Limited creates the Ford Motor Company of New Zealand Limited and loans it $1,585,076.91 to get under way.

~~~~~

July 20, 1936. The Northern Commercial Company Limited in Whitehorse, Yukon opens its doors to sell Fords. It will add Monarchs on December 11, 1945.

July 26, 1936. King Edward VIII dedicates the memorial at Vimy Ridge, a monument to Canadians who died in the Great War. Some 10,000 are on hand for the occasion.

~~~~~

November 25, 1936. Germany, Italy and Japan sign a formal alliance to protect each other in case of attack.

~~~~~

November 27, 1936. Revell Motors Sales Limited is the newest business to open on Main Street in Verona, Ontario. The automobile of choice is Ford.

~~~~~

December 6, 1936. The Canadian Broadcasting Corporation comes into being. It replaces the Canadian Radio Broadcasting Commission. The CBC will broadcast six hours a day in French and English.

~~~~~

December 10, 1936. McCulloch's Garage in Acme, Alberta has been a Ford dealer for ten years. As of today, it changes hands and will be known as Acme Garage. Relieved townspeople are happy to know that the new owners will still handle Fords.

~~~~~

December 11, 1936. King Edward VIII stuns the nation in a live radio address carried on the CBC as he announces he will step down from the throne for the woman he loves.

~~~~~

December 31, 1936. Exactly 80 Ford cars and 40 Ford trucks have been imported from Canada into Newfoundland.

December 31, 1936. The final count shows that 42,681 passenger cars have been produced during this year, including a handful of Lincolns.

~~~~~

June 8, 1937. H.H. Dier hangs out his shingle. Everybody in Mackin, Saskatchewan now knows there's a Ford dealer in town.

~~~~~

July 30, 1937. Trans-Canada Air makes its first flight from Montreal to Vancouver. Transport Minister C.D. Howe is among the passengers on the eighteen-hour flight. TCA will hire stewardesses. The women must be no taller than 5'3" and be registered nurses. They will make $140 a month but have to buy their own uniforms.

~~~~~

August 22, 1937. The CBC will now broadcast sixteen hours a day.

~~~~~

October 25, 1937. A brand new house in the Northwest End of Halifax carries a $4,100 price tag. It features hot water heating and hardwood floors. An older six-room home on Salter Street costs $500.

~~~~~

November 18, 1937. Governor-General Lord Tweedsmuir hands out the first of the Governor-General's Awards for literature in Ottawa. It becomes an annual event, honouring the best of the country's writers.

King George IV & Queen Elizabeth in a 1939 Lincoln

June 18, 1938. *The Vancouver Sun* reports that the new Ford factory in Burnaby, British Columbia has an air-conditioned lunch room for workers. The assembly plant will turn out Ford cars and trucks as well as Monarchs. The plant will be closed in 1946 and sold in 1960. The site will become home to the Metro Town Shopping Centre.

~ ~ ~ ~ ~

August 18, 1938. U.S. President Franklin Delano Roosevelt is in Kingston, Ontario to receive an honourary doctorate from Queen's University. Roosevelt tells the 5,000 in the audience that America will assist Canada if it is attacked.

December 14, 1938. The Great Depression is not over. *The Chatham Times* advises mothers that a bottle of cough syrup can be stretched into three by mixing two tablespoons of sugar to a half teacup of water and then stirring in a bottle of Buckley's Cough Mixture.

~ ~ ~ ~ ~

May 2, 1939. The National Film Board is established. It won't take long before the NFB earns its first Oscar in Hollywood.

~ ~ ~ ~ ~

May 17, 1939. King George VI and Queen Elizabeth arrive in Quebec City. They are first sovereigns to step foot on Canadian soil. Their Majesties will tour the country for a month and Canadians will love every minute of the pomp and pageantry.

~ ~ ~ ~ ~

July 12, 1939. Ladies in Toronto can take advantage of the July Special at J. Nelson Day Limited. The Yonge Street salon offers 'guaranteed permanent waves' for only $3.50.

~ ~ ~ ~ ~

August 1939. *Canadian Motorist* reports that there are some 70,000 miles of roads throughout Ontario, all of them covered with emergency roadside assistance from the Ontario Motor League. The OML will become part of the Canadian Automobile Association in the 1960s.

~ ~ ~ ~ ~

September 7, 1939. Prime Minister Mackenzie King recalls Parliament from summer recess to determine Canada's role in World War Two. Debate The House of Commons will consider the matter for three days.

September 10, 1939. Members of Parliament vote overwhelmingly to enter World War Two.

~~~~~

September 12, 1939. Parliament hikes taxes to pay for the war.

~~~~~

September 16, 1939. The first convoy of troops and supplies leave "an undisclosed eastern Canadian seaport" in order to keep the enemy off balance. In reality, that seaport is Halifax.

~~~~~

October 8, 1939. It is too late to cancel, so the National Motor Show opens in Toronto. The event has to be advanced by a week because the 200,000-square foot building, on the grounds of the Canadian National Exhibition, has been requisitioned by the Royal Canadian Army to billet troops.

~~~~~

November 24, 1939. Specials at the Safeway stores in Edmonton include Mayfair butter, three pounds for 89 cents; Airway coffee, 39 cents a pound; Aylmer's tomato soup, two 10 and-one-half ounce tins for 15 cents and 10-pound bags of granulated sugar for 72 cents. Side bacon is selling for 25 cents a pound and young local veal shoulder roast costs 12 cents a pound.

~~~~~

April 5, 1940. Stockholders at Ford are advised that the war will reduce profitability since 42 percent of the Canadian company's sales are to its subsidiaries.

April 25, 1940. Women in Quebec can now vote in provincial elections.

~~~~~

July 4, 1940. The government declares Jehovah's Witnesses to be an illegal organization because of their pacifism.

Scout Car

July 11, 1940. Unemployment Insurance comes into force.

~~~~~

August 5, 1940. Camillien Houde, Mayor of Montreal is arrested by police as he leaves City Hall. His crime is his opposition to the war.

A ugust 23, 1940. Naturalized Canadians born in Germany and Italy who became citizens after September 1, 1922 are stripped of their citizenship and must report to police as enemy aliens.

~~~~~

S eptember 1940. Tens of thousands flock to Toronto to see the new 1941 models at the National Automobile Show, held in the Automotive Building on the grounds of the CNE. Most of the Ford exhibit is made up of the ten different types of army vehicles that the company is building for the Canadian and other Empire governments. Officials for Ford report that the company has orders for 50,000 war machines and is turning out 400 units a day at the Windsor plant.

~~~~~

N ovember 20, 1940. In Vancouver, folks are lining up at The Plaza and Paradise theatres to see Charlie Chaplin in his new comedy, *The Great Dictator*. Matinees are 75 cents and full price is $1.10 after five o'clock.

~~~~~

N ovember 22, 1940. People in Calgary are heading down to the Heintzman and Company Limited at 329 Eighth Avenue West to see the new, All Canadian Heintzman Airline eight-tube parlour radios. The Heintzmans feature a "Super-Sensitive Tuning Eye," AM and Shortwave channels and even offer phonograph and FM jacks all for $144.50!

~~~~~

J anuary 1, 1941. The Dominion Bureau of Statistics counts noses this year. There are 11.5 million of us stretched out from Cape Breton to the Yukon.

January 8, 1941. Formerly the Ford dealer in Montague, Prince Edward Island, S.R. Johnson opens the doors to a new dealership in Charlottetown. It will be closed on December 22, 1942 when Johnson joins the Royal Canadian Army. After serving King and Country with honour, he will return to the Garden Province to open a new Ford and Monarch dealership on May 28, 1946.

~~~~~

March 27, 1941. Stockholders learn that 1940 was the company's best year ever. Sales were up 55 percent over 1939, 97,360 units were sold. Much of the increase was for motor vehicles for military purposes by His Majesty's Governments in Canada, the United Kingdom and other British Empire countries.

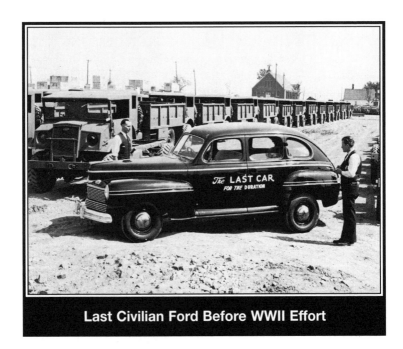

Last Civilian Ford Before WWII Effort

October 18, 1941. Ottawa institutes the Wartime Prices and Trade Board. The government watchdog agency is also in charge of rationing.

~~~~~

December 7, 1941. Parliament declares war on Imperial Japan.

~~~~~

February 1942. Ford discontinues assembly of automobiles in its Toronto plant.

~~~~~

February 24, 1942. Lucy Maude Montgomery is dead. The author of *Anne of Green Gables* is 68.

~~~~~

February 26, 1942. Ottawa announces that Japanese-Canadians will be interred in camps or removed from the West Coast. 21,000 people are displaced.

~~~~~

March 31, 1942. The last civilian Ford is built in Windsor, Ontario. The company will dedicate its considerable resources to winning the war.

~~~~~

April 10, 1942. The value of the Ford plant in Malaya has been reduced to $1.00 since the Japanese Imperial Army now occupies Singapore and the factory has ceased production.

April 27, 1942. Charles Sorensen is appointed to the board.

~ ~ ~ ~ ~

June 21, 1942. A Japanese submarine fires at the Estevan Point lighthouse on the coast of Vancouver Island. There are no casualties.

~ ~ ~ ~ ~

June 28, 1942. J.E. Porter, general superintendent of manufacturing operations, board member and VP dies. He has been with the company since 1922.

~ ~ ~ ~ ~

August 19, 1942. A total of 993 Canadian soldiers are killed and 1,874 taken prisoner at Dieppe, one of the most disastrous battles of the war.

~ ~ ~ ~ ~

October 15, 1942. A U-boat torpedoes the Newfoundland ferry, on its way to North Sydney. A total of 137 are dead including 31 crew members. Fortunately, 101 survived the sinking of the *Caribou*.

~ ~ ~ ~ ~

November 20, 1942. The Alcan Military Highway opens. It stretches from Dawson Creek, British Columbia to Fairbanks, Alaska.

~ ~ ~ ~ ~

December 31, 1942. Five cars are exported to Newfoundland under the emergency civilian defense programme. The YMCA is granted permission to purchase three Panel Delivery pickups and a station wagon. The Knights of Columbus is granted permission to buy a Super Station Wagon.

May 26, 1943. Edsel B. Ford, Chairman of the Board dies.

~~~~~

July 10, 1943. The First Canadian Division invades Sicily.

114-Inch
STAKE

1943 Stake Truck

August 15, 1943. Joint Canadian and American forces take the Alaskan island of Kiska from the Japanese Imperial Army.

~~~~~

August 17, 1943. The Quesnel brothers buy Lake Motors Limited in Williams Lake, British Columbia. It is an act of faith, the boys won't have any new Fords to sell until 1946.

September 8, 1943. Italy surrenders to the Allies. That doesn't mean that the war is over, two German divisions are immediately deployed to Italy.

~~~~~

September 15, 1943. Henry Ford is elected chairman of the board.

~~~~~

September 29, 1943. The first synthetic rubber is produced at the Polymer Corporation Limited in Sarnia, Ontario.

~~~~~

December 31, 1943. Two trucks was the total number of Ford vehicles released to civilians in Newfoundland for the year.

~~~~~

March 28, 1944. Stephen Leacock is dead at the age of 74. The humour author penned more than 25 books and won the Governor-General's Award in 1937.

~~~~~

March 30, 1944. Figures released that total civilian output of all cars, trucks and tractors for the 1943 calendar year totaled 3,511 units.

~~~~~

April 20, 1944. Nearly 14,000 workers walk off the job at Ford. Their leaders claim that Ford wants to "smash" the union. The National Wartime Labour Relations Board refuses to negotiate until the workers stop picketing. The strike will end on May 10.

April 24, 1944. Henry Ford II is elected a director of the company and becomes a VP on June 30th.

Child Guests Arrive from Britain

May 1, 1944. The Wartime Prices and Trade Board announces that coffee and tea rations will be doubled to eight ounces of tea or 32 ounces of coffee every thirty days.

~~~~~

June 6, 1944. More than 175,000 Allied soldiers storm the beaches of Normandy. It is D-Day for France. Here at home, Hoskins Ford Sales Limited inks a deal to serve the residents of Smithers, British Columbia.

December 31, 1944. A total of 18 Fords has been released for sale in Newfoundland during the year. Five Super Deluxe Fordors were shipped to Corner Brook and two to St. John's. A further eleven trucks were permitted to be sold to civilians in need.

~~~~~

January 31, 1945. The last of the 'Child Guests' leaves Windsor, Ontario on the CPR. They are headed home to Britain. The 123 children's parents work for Ford in the UK. They came to Canada in 1940 to escape the bombings and stayed in the homes of Ford of Canada employees.

~~~~~

February 18, 1945. The cheque is in the mail. Ottawa mails out the first ever monthly baby bonus, better known as the Mother's allowance cheques.

~~~~~

March 2, 1945. Artist Emily Carr is dead. The British Columbia painter was eccentric, right down to the monkey in the pram but her artistic legacy is one of the finest the world has ever seen.

~~~~~

March 18, 1945. Maurice "Rocket" Richard scores 50 goals in 50 games. Rocket's big 5-0 takes place in Beantown as the Habs trounce the Bruins four to two in the final game of the season.

~~~~~

March 24, 1945. Allied soldiers have crossed the Rhine River and are now inside The Third Reich.

March 29, 1945. It is revealed that the total number of cars, trucks and tractors released to civilians throughout the country during 1944 was 5,980.

~ ~ ~ ~ ~

April 16, 1945. A German submarine torpedoes the *HMCS Esquimalt* just outside of Halifax harbour. Of the crew, 39 are dead.

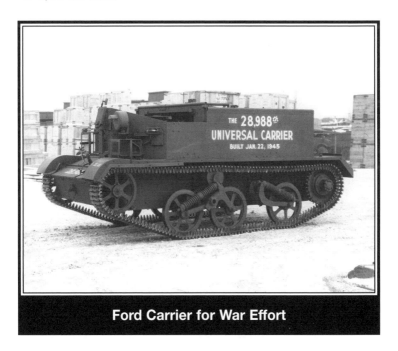

THE 28,988th
UNIVERSAL CARRIER
BUILT JAN. 22, 1945

Ford Carrier for War Effort

May 4, 1945. The 1st Canadian Paratroop Battalion meets the Russian Army at Wismar, Germany.

~ ~ ~ ~ ~

May 7, 1945. Adolf Hitler commits suicide. He orders his chauffeur to burn his body in gasoline to prevent desecration by the Allies.

May 7, 1945. Victory celebrations get out of hand in Halifax as people riot. Two people are killed and much of the central business district is trashed.

May 18, 1945. Prime Minister Mackenzie King tells a crowd in Edmonton that some 45,000 troops will be re-deployed to the Pacific Theatre to fight the Japanese.

~~~~~

May 22, 1945. Ottawa warns citizens in British Columbia and Alberta to be on the lookout for huge balloons released by Japan and carried across the Pacific on the jet stream. The balloons carry deadly bombs that contain anthrax or bubonic plague.

First Post-War Civilian Ford

May 23, 1945. McBride, British Columbia gets a new Ford-Monarch dealership as Shovar Motors opens. There won't be any new cars to sell until rationing ends, however.

~~~~~

June 7, 1945. The Royal Canadian Navy releases figures that its ships have escorted 25,343 merchant ships to the UK during the war and that 1,900 sailors have died for King and Country.

~~~~~

August 6, 1945. An atomic bomb is dropped on Hiroshima, Japan and 80,000 people are dead.

~~~~~

August 14, 1945. The war is over, Japan has surrendered. Ford of Canada has built 336,187 army trucks of every imaginable variety and 33,992 Universal and Windsor carriers. 82 percent of the factory was dedicated to war work and 18 percent was set aside for essential home front needs.

~~~~~

September 12, 1945. Ford wraps up its military contracts to His Majesty's Governments and to the Dominion Government.

~~~~~

September 12, 1945. Workers in Windsor go on strike. It is a long and bitter strike that will drag on until December 19, 1945.

~~~~~

November 2, 1945. Strike or not, the Ford sign goes up in the Weston suburb of Toronto as Cruikshank Motors Limited gears up for a peacetime, post-war world.

November 11, 1945. It is Remembrance Day. Workers at Ford of Canada may be walking the picket line but they will pause at the eleventh hour of the eleventh day of the eleventh month to remember the 5,787 employees who served with His Majesty's Royal Canadian forces. They will especially remember the 146 co-workers who gave their lives for King and Country.

~ ~ ~ ~ ~

December 31, 1945. The war is over but rationing continues. A total of eight passenger cars and 46 trucks were released to civilians in Newfoundland during the year.

Monarch Introduction

January 14, 1946. The first post-war Ford is built in Windsor. It is announced that Mercury and Lincoln will be split off as a new dealer network, separate from Ford dealers. The move doubles the number of dealerships across the country.

January 29 1946. Justice Ivan Rand of the Supreme Court has arbitrated the Ford strike. He rules that the UAW can not have a closed shop at Ford but that all workers must pay union dues.

~~~~~

March 20, 1946. Executives announce a new truck line. Mercury trucks are for Canada only and will offer light and heavy duty models through Lincoln-Mercury dealers in all nine provinces. Folks can see them at the dealer on Saturday, March 23.

~~~~~

March 23, 1946. Monarch is introduced. The country's 750 Ford dealers are delighted to make room for the medium-priced cars on their showroom floors, especially since they lost the Mercury and Lincoln lines.

~~~~~

April 13, 1946. Figures show that 48,881 Ford cars and trucks (including 1,585 tractors) were sold and shipped during 1945.

~~~~~

April 29, 1946. Wallace R. Campbell moves from President to Chairman of the Board. Douglas Greig becomes president.

~~~~~

May 7, 1946. Residents of Kaladar, Ontario are pleased that Bence Motor Sales Limited has opened up as a Ford and Monarch dealership.

~~~~~

August 1946. The 2 millionth Canadian Ford is built.

November 30, 1946.   The War Labour Board is disbanded. Ottawa is ready to let the unions and the private sector sort out wages and working conditions alone.

~~~~~

December 4, 1946.   The City of Toronto retires the last 25 Clydesdales used to haul garbage. They are replaced with trucks.

~~~~~

December 18, 1946.   The Wartime Prices and Trade Board grants a 10 percent increase in retail prices on passenger cars and 7 percent on commercial vehicles. Ford will lower its prices on all Ford, Monarch and Mercury cars and Ford and Mercury trucks by $35 in March of 1947.

~~~~~

January 1, 1947.   Canada is no longer a British colony. We will not be classified as 'Britons born abroad' nor will we carry British passports anymore. As of today we are Canadians, citizens of an independent, sovereign nation.

~~~~~

April 7, 1947.   Henry Ford is dead. Ironically, he will be taken to his final resting place in a Packard hearse.

~~~~~

May 6, 1947.   Folks who live in Nova Scotia's smallest county have their very own Ford and Monarch dealer as Keltic Motors Limited opens in Antigonish.

August 10, 1947. Wallace R. Campbell is dead. The Chairman of the Board and former president of Ford of Canada, Limited was with the company for 42 years.

~ ~ ~ ~ ~

October 6, 1947. D'Astous Motors Limited is ready to sell Fords and Monarchs to friends and neighbours who live along the Restigouche River in Atholville, New Brunswick.

1947 Mercury

February 13, 1947. Imperial Oil has struck black gold with its Leduc Number One well in Leduc, Alberta. It is the second in a string of gushers that will make Alberta a "have" province.

July 22, 1947. The country's first nuclear reactor comes on line in Chalk River, Ontario.

~ ~ ~ ~ ~

November 19, 1947. Ford is obliged to raise prices on passenger cars by as much as $144 to $216 in order to pay increased excise taxes to Ottawa.

~ ~ ~ ~ ~

November 18, 1947. Before today consumers paid an 8 percent sales tax and a 10 percent excise tax on the wholesale cost of the car. Now the consumer pays a 25 percent excise tax on passenger cars up to $1,200, 50 percent on the part of the price between $1,200 and $2,000 and 75 percent excise tax on anything over $2,000. Yesterday, a new Ford Super Deluxe Fordor cost $279 in taxes, today Ottawa pockets $368.49.

~ ~ ~ ~ ~

December 31, 1947. A total of 314 Ford cars and trucks were exported to Newfoundland during the calendar year.

~ ~ ~ ~ ~

December 31, 1947. The Canadian Ambassador to Washington will find it easier to get around the city now that he has received his smart, new Mercury Town Sedan.

~ ~ ~ ~ ~

December 31, 1947. 60,777 passenger cars were sold by Ford-Monarch and Lincoln-mercury dealers. That is 26.2 percent of all cars sold in the Dominion. Ford is the number one truck seller with 29.4 percent of the market. 101,185 vehicles are built of which 40.6 percent are shipped abroad. The only Ford vehicles imported into Canada for the year were 182 Ford buses and 235 Lincoln automobiles.

January 1948. A shortage of natural gas causes the Windsor plant to shut down for 17 days during the first eight weeks of the year.

~~~~~

January 1, 1948. Ford of Canada is about to have its best year ever. Sales will hit 63,955 car and truck units. That includes 1,295 British Fords. Production of cars, trucks buses and tractors will reach 107,397 units. Wages of $40 million will be paid out to 14,298 employees. On a sad note, the Vancouver assembly plant, in operation since 1935 is closed. Ford is the largest auto manufacturer in the country and the largest exporter of automobiles.

1949 Meteor

January 6, 1948. Wilmot Hatheway opens a Ford and Monarch dealership in Bathurst, New Brunswick.

February 6, 1948. Barbara Ann Scott of Ottawa wins Olympic gold for figure skating at the Winter Olympics in St. Moritz, Switzerland.

~~~~~

February 20, 1948. The Dominion Bureau of Statistics has counted up that in the country's 3.1 million homes, 90 percent of us own radios while only 50 percent of us have telephones.

~~~~~

April 15, 1948. Ford of Canada sold $149, 304,072 worth of vehicles in 1947—101,918 cars trucks and 7,800 tractors.

~~~~~

June 1948. The new Meteor is unveiled. It immediately shoots into third place, taking nearly 11 percent of all sales in Canada. All the cars in the Ford stable are so completely new that "there was nothing the same but the air in the tires."

~~~~~

June 12, 1948. The 14,500 employees at Ford of Canada accept a nine-cent-an-hour wage increase and get paid for two more statutory holidays—bringing the number of paid days off to six a year.

~~~~~

June 22, 1948. Price increases on Canadian Ford products are double those of their US counterpart, hitting 17.6 percent.

~~~~~

July 1, 1948. A supplier strike forces the Windsor plant to shut down. 5,000 workers are affected.

July 22, 1948. In a referendum, Newfoundlanders vote to join Canada rather than to be a self-governing nation. The happy event will take place on March 31, 1949.

~~~~~

August 1, 1948. Ottawa abandons the controversial sliding excise tax on passenger cars that it brought in last November. Officials at Ford heave a sigh of relief.

~~~~~

August 4, 1948. Ford cuts prices from $11 to $363 in reaction to Ottawa's decision to change the tax structure on automobiles.

1949 Ford Tudor

August 12, 1948. Prices rise on cars and trucks anywhere from $110 to $200 as a result of rising material and labour costs.

December 14, 1948. The Supreme Court of Canada rules that the Dominion Butter Board has overstepped its bounds. Consumers have the right to buy margarine. It has been illegal to purchase the butter substitute in this country since 1886.

~~~~~

December 31, 1948. Dealers sell 3,920 passenger cars imported from Ford Motor Company Limited of Dagenham, England. That is up from 1,295 vehicles the previous year.August 30, 1949 Abbotsford Motors Limited, which first began selling and servicing Fords in this British Columbia community in 1931, is now a proud new Monarch dealer, too.

~~~~~

January 15, 1949. A Royal Canadian Air Force North Star flies non-stop from Vancouver to Halifax in just eight hours and thirty-two minutes.

~~~~~

March 31, 1949. A total of 42 new Fords have been exported to Newfoundland since January 1. Today, Britain's oldest colony joins Confederation as Canada's tenth province. Officials at Ford will now shift Newfoundland from the export department to domestic sales.

~~~~~

April 4, 1949. Canada joins the North American Treaty Organization as a charter member.

~~~~~

April 28, 1949. The old British Empire gives way to the new British Commonwealth of nations. Canada is an important player.

September 1949. Ottawa devalues the dollar. Ford does not increase prices.

~~~~~

September 7, 1949. Construction begins on Toronto's subway system.

~~~~~

October 12, 1949. Hickman Motors Limited opens its doors in St. John's, Newfoundland as a Ford and Monarch dealer.

~~~~~

December 10, 1949. All the provinces, except Quebec, sign an agreement to create the Trans-Canada Highway. Quebec doesn't sign because it already has a (mostly) paved road crossing it. The new, 4,497-mile asphalt ribbon will stretch from sea to shining sea and take thirteen years to complete.

~~~~~

January 1, 1950. There are 665 Ford-Monarch dealers and 338 Lincoln-Mercury-Meteor dealers spread out from St. John's to Victoria.

~~~~~

April 5, 1950. Reardon Motors Limited is one of the nation's 356 Mercury-Lincoln-Meteor dealers. Reardon takes out an advertisement in the *Chatham Times* to welcome the Hudson Motors of Canada Limited as that company resumes post-war assembly of automobiles in nearby Tilbury.

~~~~~

May 5, 1950. Much of southern Manitoba is flooded by the Red River. An estimated 90,000 citizens will be evacuated from the affected area by week's end.

May 8, 1950. Folks walking along the 200 block of Van Norman Street in Port Arthur, Ontario can't help but notice that Jesseman Motors Limited has just opened up as a new Lincoln-Mercury-Meteor dealership.

~~~~~

June 25, 1950. The Korean War starts. It creates havoc in the car industry and Ford of Canada is caught up in the pinch, too. Steel is the first material to be affected; frames and body panels are in short supply.

~~~~~

September 1, 1950. Ottawa hikes the excise tax on automobiles from 10 percent to 15 percent. This little tax grab adds $225 to the price of a new Ford Custom Fordor sedan.

~~~~~

September 30, 1950. Ottawa cuts the dollar loose to float. It will rise in value. That turns out to be good for stockholders at Ford of Canada.

~~~~~

October 1, 1950. All workers are now covered by a company paid pension plan. Workers with 30 years' service will be paid $55 a month when they turn 65 years of age.

~~~~~

December 31, 1950. How we love those little British Fords! Canadians snapped up 14,751 of the cars from Dagenham during the year.

March 1951. The federal government imposes sharp restrictions on credit in hopes of discouraging consumer spending. This will affect people's ability to buy new Fords.

~~~~~

April 1951. Ottawa slaps a 20 percent Defense Surcharge Tax on corporations to pay for the Korean War. Ford will pay $55,885,657 in taxes this year.

~~~~~

April 1951. The excise and sales tax on cars is hiked to 35 percent of the wholesale cost. This will prompt a swift decline of sales throughout the industry. Ford will reduce schedules and lay off 4,346 workers.

~~~~~

April 30, 1951. Half of the automobiles on the nation's roads today are ten years old or older, says Rhys M. Sale, President of Ford Motor Company of Canada, Limited.

~~~~~

October 5, 1951. West Park Motors opens its doors in Corner Brook, Newfoundland as a Ford and Monarch dealer.

~~~~~

December 3, 1951. A wildcat strike shuts down factory operations at Ford. Without heat, extensive damage is done to the plants. The strike ends on December 14 but repairs will mean that production can't begin again until Boxing Day.

~~~~~

January 24, 1952. Vincent Massey is named Governor-General. He is the first Canadian-born person to be the King's representative in Ottawa.

February 6, 1952.   King George VI dies in his sleep. His daughter Elizabeth will reign in his stead.

~~~~~

May 1, 1952. The first steel girders go up for the new assembly plant in Oakville, Ontario.

~~~~~

September 6, 1952. The CBC makes the big leap from radio to TV. The country's first television station takes to the airwaves as Montrealers warm up their Northern Electrics, turn the dial to Channel Six and watch CBMT sign on. Programming is bilingual in the nation's largest city.

~~~~~

September 8, 1952. No longer do they have to watch TV stations from Buffalo, New York, Torontonians now have CBC Television as they tune in to CBLT for the first time.

~~~~~

November 26, 1952. Brown Brothers Ford opens for business in Vancouver.

~~~~~

December 11, 1952. Dealers right across the country throw open the doors as Canadians flock to see the new 1953 Lincoln, Meteor and Mercury lineups.

~~~~~

December 12, 1952. Ford dealers proudly show off the new 1953 Ford and Monarch lines.

New Oakville Assembly Plant

January 16, 1953. Ford's truck lines will be down for four weeks as workers change over to new models.

~~~~~

February 14, 1953. Ford adds a Saturday shift to get cars into the hands of eager consumers.

~~~~~

February 19, 1953. Aspol Motors joins the Ford family in Dawson Creek, British Columbia. There will be a fair number of block heater sales to keep those Fords and Monarchs warm.

March 3, 1953. Lawrence Steele opens the newest Ford Monarch dealership in North Sydney, Nova Scotia.

~~~~~

May 11, 1953. The first passenger car rolls out the doors of the new Oakville plant. The plant is huge, 32.5 acres under one roof. It will take fifteen months for all assembly to be transferred from Windsor.

~~~~~

June 2, 1953 . Queen Elizabeth II is crowned. RCMP officers take part in her coronation. Millions watch on the CBC as the tapes are flown by the RCAF to Canada for broadcast.

1954 Monarch

June 4, 1953. Power steering and power brakes become optional on Monarch and Mercury cars.

~~~~~

December 10, 1953. A day-and-a-half is lost in Windsor because of a $100,000 fire in the trim department.

~~~~~

December 16, 1953. Canadians flock to dealerships to see the new 1954 Mercury lineup.

~~~~~

December 17, 1953. The new 1954 Monarchs are unveiled at dealerships across Canada.

~~~~~

January 1954. The new Oakville Assembly Plant administration office is opened. There are 1,003 dealers selling and servicing Ford products from St. John's to Victoria.

~~~~~

May 1954. The last passenger car is assembled in Windsor. The plant will be refitted to produce a new overhead valve V-8 engine.

~~~~~

May 12, 1954. The Ford Motor Company of India, Limited is liquidated because its government regulations make it impossible to do business in that Commonwealth country. Profit from the sale is returned to Ford of Canada, the Indian company's parent.

May 13, 1954. Canada and the United States sign an agreement to build the St. Lawrence Seaway.

~ ~ ~ ~ ~

August 16, 1954. It is announced that truck assembly has moved completely from Windsor to Oakville.

~ ~ ~ ~ ~

August 17, 1954. The nation's oldest auto manufacturer turns fifty today. Ford pulls out all the stops to celebrate. Two out of every five Canadian-built vehicles on the road boast the blue oval. Ford has built 41 percent of the seven million cars produced in this country. A total of 2,888,692 cars and trucks have been built in Canadian factories. The company has operated at a profit for 45 of its 50 years. Only in 1928, 1931, 1932, 1933 and 1946 were there net losses.

~ ~ ~ ~ ~

August 27, 1954. McQuaig Motors Limited on Wellington Street West in Chatham, Ontario has only eleven used cars on the lot. Among the cars that "must be sold immediately!" is a 1947 Mercury sedan. The asking price is $395.

~ ~ ~ ~ ~

September 9, 1954. Sixteen-year old Marilyn Bell becomes the first person to swim the 52 kilometres across Lake Ontario. More than 250,000 fans are on hand to celebrate her victory when she swims into Toronto Harbour.

~ ~ ~ ~ ~

September 25, 1954. *The National Post* reports that Canadians now own nearly 400,000 television sets.

October 10, 1954. The company is crippled by a prolonged strike. 14,758 workers will stay off the job until January 30, 1955. Sales will be 20 percent lower than in 1953.

~ ~ ~ ~ ~

October 15, 1954. Hurricane Hazel hits Toronto. With winds of up to 120 kilometres an hour, the storm kills 81 people and leaves 4,000 homeless.

~ ~ ~ ~ ~

April 1955. The federal government reduces personal income tax by 5 percent and lowers the taxes on cars, too. Ford will jump from 96,385 sales to 120,465 cars this year. That will include 4,009 units imported from the UK and 2,191 cars imported from the US.

~ ~ ~ ~ ~

April 2, 1955. The Angus L. Macdonald Bridge opens between Halifax and Dartmouth. It is the second longest suspension bridge in the Commonwealth. Only the Lion's Gate Bridge in Vancouver is longer.

~ ~ ~ ~ ~

June 25, 1955. Ontario has completed and paved 319.2 miles of its 1,412-mile stretch of the Trans-Canada Highway.

~ ~ ~ ~ ~

January 3, 1956. Hometown Service Limited hangs out its shingle in Winnipeg. That beautiful new Thunderbird on the showroom floor retails for $3,798 plus taxes.

June 30, 1956. Manitobans buy 6,689 new Fords, 4,513 new Meteors, 1,161 new Mercurys, 1,036 new Monarchs and 162 new Lincolns. Many of these fine vehicles will be seen at the nation's first A&W drive-in that just opened in Winnipeg.

~ ~ ~ ~ ~

October 31, 1956. *The Ford Graphic* reports that more than 25,000 people in Montreal came to the unveiling of the Lincoln-Mercury-Meteor models held in the St. Laurent Arena. Visitors attending the four-day gala got to meet the Alouettes who will lose the Grey Cup to Edmonton for the second year in a row.

~ ~ ~ ~ ~

December 31, 1956. Only 3,645 Fords were imported from Britain this year. Demand is high but there is a shortage of vehicles as the Dagenham plant changes over to new models. There is a world-wide shortage of container ships to boot.

~ ~ ~ ~ ~

April 2, 1957. Elvis Presley performs for 24,000 fans at Maple Leaf Gardens in Toronto.

~ ~ ~ ~ ~

June 21, 1957. John Diefenbaker and his Tories are sworn in to power by the Governor-General. Ellen Fairclough is the first woman to be a cabinet minister. The chartered accountant is Secretary of State and will be permitted to bow like her cabinet colleagues, not curtsey, when the Queen visits.

~ ~ ~ ~ ~

October 4, 1957. The Russians are watching! The Soviet Union touches off the space race as its *Sputnik* satellite is launched.

1958 Edsel

October 14, 1957. Lester B. Pearson receives the Nobel Peace Prize. The World War Two spy will become prime minister in 1963.

~~~~~

October 31, 1957. The first portion of the Trans-Canada Highway is complete. Motorists can drive completely across all 406 miles of Saskatchewan on the freshly paved Number One Highway.

~~~~~

December 31, 1957. Canada is in recession. Sales of British Fords are up sharply to 5,263 units at the expense of larger cars. Total passenger car sales for the year is down to 123,407 units.

September 6, 1958. The National Capital Commission is created. Ottawa and Hull will reflect the country's flavour.

~~~~~

October 1, 1958. Employees at Ford accept a 6-cent an hour pay rise.

~~~~~

November 1958. Canadians don't like the Edsel. We want our homegrown Monarch back. The 'King of the Road' makes its second appearance this month, reincarnated as Monarch Mark II.

~~~~~

December 19, 1958. High River, Alberta gets a new Ford-Edsel-Monarch dealer as High River Motor Company Limited opens its doors.

~~~~~

December 31, 1958. Sales of Ford, Meteor, Edsel Mercury and Lincoln passenger cars will be 91,545 this year. It is down because of the recession. 86 percent of the cars sold are made in Canada. Another 9,109 Fords come from Britain and 2,056 Thunderbirds, Lincolns and Continentals are imported from the USA.

~~~~~

June 26, 1959. Queen Elizabeth, Prime Minister Diefenbaker and US President Dwight Eisenhower are in Montreal to officially open the St. Lawrence Seaway. Balloons, fireworks and flags delight the crowds.

July 22, 1959. Universal Sales & Service Limited opens under new management on 5th Avenue SW in Calgary. The company, which has been around since 1921, will continue to sell Lincoln-Mercury-Meteors and Taunus as well as the all-new, all-Canadian Frontenac.

~~~~~

August 1, 1959. Major-General Georges Vanier is appointed Governor-General. He is the second Canadian born GG and the first Francophone to be head of state.

~~~~~

October 8, 1959. Canadians can see the new 1960 Ford lineup, including the new compact Frontenac and Falcon. The new small cars will compete with the 12,527 imports from Ford's German and British subsidiaries.

~~~~~

November 1, 1959. Ford workers will find more in their pay cheques as they receive a 6-cent an hour pay rise.

~~~~~

November 19, 1959. The Edsel is discontinued after 2,846 of the 1960 models were built—all of them in Louisville, Kentucky. Canadians prefer Monarchs and prove it by buying 4,958 of them.

~~~~~

March 10, 1960. Native Canadians are given the right to vote in federal elections.

April 14, 1960. The Montreal Canadiens win their fifth Stanley Cup in a row.

~ ~ ~ ~ ~

August 1960. A camera crew arrives in Vancouver on a cross-country trek from Halifax in the new 1961 Frontenac only to learn that the Canada-only compact has been pulled from the domestic market in favour of the Mercury Comet.

~ ~ ~ ~ ~

September 30, 1960. People in Robervale, Quebec get a new car dealer as L.G. Automobile Limitée hangs up its Ford and Monarch sign.

~ ~ ~ ~ ~

October 1960. A federally appointed Royal Commission has concluded its hearings into the flood of imported vehicles pouring into the country. Ford officials await the report to the Government in the summer of 1961.

~ ~ ~ ~ ~

December 1, 1960. Employees at Ford get a pay rise of 6 cents an hour.

~ ~ ~ ~ ~

December 15, 1960. Dorval Airport opens in this Montreal suburb. The $30 million facility will serve the nation's largest city well.

~ ~ ~ ~ ~

December 31, 1960. Stockholders learn that Ford of Canada owns three new subsidiaries: Ford Motor Company of Rhodesia (Private) Limited; Ford of Canada-Bermuda Company Limited and Ford of Canada (Jamaica) Company Limited.

1961 Frontenac Prototype

May 1961. Ford's new glass fabricating plant near Niagara Falls is dedicated and open for business.

~~~~~

May 1961. The official opening of Ford's new headquarters is held in Oakville.

~~~~~

June 21, 1961. The federal government drops the hated excise tax on new automobiles. Buyers appreciate it, especially those who are buying a new Monarch. After this year, the grand name will be retired.

~~~~~

August 3, 1961. The New Democratic Party is born from the CCF and the Canadian Labour Congress. Firebrand Tommy Douglas is elected leader.

October 1, 1961. The CBC has competition as a new kid hits the airwaves. The Canadian Television Network (CTN) begins broadcasting. It boasts affiliates in Winnipeg (CJAY-TV), Calgary (CFCN-TV), Vancouver (CHAN-TV), Toronto (CFTO-TV), Ottawa (CJOH-TV), Montreal (CFCF-TV) and Halifax (CJCH-TV). The privately owned broadcaster will change its name to CTV within a year.

~~~~~

January 15, 1962. A new agreement is signed with the UAW in Canada. Workers will get a rise of 6 cents an hour of 2.5 per-cent--whichever is greater—each year over the next three years. There are changes in the insurance plan and pension benefits, too.

~~~~~

March 18, 1962. There are so many orders for new Fords that the plant in Oakville starts a second shift. 1,400 new men will be hired.

~~~~~

March 31, 1962. Rhys M. Sale retires from a lifetime of service to Ford. He will step down from being chairman of the board but stay on as a director.

~~~~~

April 1962. The board of directors votes to spend $15 million to upgrade the foundry in Windsor.

~~~~~

April 1, 1962. Saskatchewan adopts universal Medicare but it will cost an extra $12 a head in taxes.

June 1962. New tariffs from Ottawa prompt the decline of imported Fords as sales drop by 3,924 units to only 5,505.

~~~~~

September 3, 1962. Prime Minister Diefenbaker officially opens the Trans-Canada Highway at Rogers Pass, British Columbia. The national artery stretches 7,700 kilometres from St. John's to Victoria. Paving will take a couple more years. In Newfoundland, big signs along the gravel road will read, "With Pearson, We'll finish the drive in '65."

~~~~~

September 25, 1962. The first Canadian satellite, *Allouette*, is shot into space. Once in orbit, it will help immensely in speeding inter-provincial communications.

~~~~~

November 1, 1962. Ottawa drops the 25 percent import duty on automatic transmissions. This is good for Ford owners.

~~~~~

November 2, 1962. Fort Motors Limited is Ford's newest home, located in Fort St. John, British Columbia.

~~~~~

December 31, 1962. Sales of passenger cars for Ford are up this year to 121, 257 units, 22,802 trucks and 2,763 tractors.

~~~~~

May 17, 1963. A series of explosions occur in Westmount, Quebec as seventeen letter bombs are discovered. A group called the *Front de liberation du Quebec* (FLQ) may be involved. It seeks independence from Canada.

May 31, 1963. We purchased 57,489 new cars this month, an average of 2,111 a day.

~~~~~

July 26, 1963. *Bluenose II* is launched in Lunenburg, Nova Scotia. The schooner is a replica of the country's most famous--and the world's fastest--saltbanker. The original ship was wrecked off the coast of Haiti in 1946.

~~~~~

July 31, 1963. Dealers have sold 133,672 Fords, Meteors, Mercurys and Lincolns and wrap up the year with 26.4 percent of all sales across the Canada.

1965 Mustang

September 23, 1963. For $3, folks can see *Lawrence of Arabia* at the Fairlawn Theatre at the corner of Yonge and Fairlawn in Toronto. Matinees are $2. This is the tenth and final week to see Jack Lemmon and Shirley MacLaine in *Irma la Douce* at Loew's Uptown on Yonge and Bloor.

~~~~~

April 17, 1964. The Mustang is introduced. Canadian President Karl Scott notes that while the cars are built in the US, their engines, drive trains and other components are made in Windsor.

~~~~~

August 1964. Construction begins on a new truck assembly plant in Oakville. When complete it will boast a million square feet under its roof.

Ontario Truck Plant Opens

September 6, 1964. The Beatles arrive in Toronto. The pop group is met at the airport by 3,000 adoring fans.

~~~~~

October 7, 1964. Cam-Don Motors opens in Perdue, Saskatchewan with the intention of selling and servicing Fords.

~~~~~

November 1964. Operations in Oakville are suspended because strikes by Ford workers in the US have caused the Canadian plant to run out of components.

~~~~~

January 16, 1965. Prime Minister Pearson and US President Johnson sign Auto Pact. The historic agreement allows duty free trans-shipment of automotive parts and completed vehicles into each other's markets.

~~~~~

February 15, 1965. The Red Ensign is lowered from flagpoles across the nation for the last time. A new flag—one with two red bars on the ends and a large red maple leaf in the centre of a white field—is the nation's new flag. The maple leaf forever!

~~~~~

August 1965. The new, $25 million Ontario Truck Plant opens in Oakville. It covers a million square feet of space.

~~~~~

March 4, 1966. The nation's first parliamentary sex scandal erupts when Gerda Munsinger's name is raised in the House of Commons. Former cabinet ministers in Diefenbaker's Conservative government are accused of having had affairs with the woman who is alleged to be a spy for East Germany. Maybe all Ms. Munsinger wanted was her 'bedtime Tories.'

~~~~~

April 4, 1966. A second shift is necessary at the truck plant in Oakville. 500 men are hired, bringing the total of workers to 1,617.

~~~~~

August 12, 1966. Dupuis Ford Lincoln Incorporated is what the new sign says on rue St-Isadore in Casselman, Ontario. That is good news for Ford and Lincoln owners in the neighbourhood.

~~~~~

December 31, 1966. The country's 805 Ford dealers have new signs to put up. 215 dealers have them already, it will take three years for the programme to be completed.

~~~~~

December 31, 1966. Prime Minister Pearson lights the Centennial flame on Parliament Hill to start the year-long festivities as Canada celebrates its 100th birthday.

~~~~~

January 1, 1967. Television goes from black and white to colour with Parliament's blessing.

~~~~~

January 7, 1967. The Centennial Train leaves Victoria, British Columbia for a year-long trek across the country. The mobile museum will delight millions.

April 27, 1967. The World's Fair opens in Montreal. More than 50 million will visit Expo 67 on the island made from dirt dug up from the city's new Metro system.

~~~~~

June 20, 1967. Prime Minister Pearson dedicates the Library of Canada.

1968 Meteor Lemoyne

December 18, 1967. The $65 million St. Thomas, Ontario assembly plant opens. Its workers build Ford Falcons for the North American market. It is officially dedicated by Henry Ford II.

~~~~~

April 12, 1968. New Brunswick becomes the country's first officially bilingual province.

~~~~~

April 22, 1968. Rhys M. Sale retires from the board of directors. He has been with Ford of Canada since 1915 and served in World War One.

June 6, 1968. The St. Thomas plant throws an open house in which government, business and community leaders participate.

~~~~~

June 24, 1968. Pierre Elliot Trudeau and his Grits sweep the federal election. The press describes voters' enthusiastic response to the charismatic politician as 'Trudeaumania.'

~~~~~

July 1, 1968. National Medicare becomes law. Canadians now have free access to medical services.

~~~~~

July 22, 1968. The St. Boniface Basilica is destroyed by fire. Winnipeggers of all faiths will miss the historic landmark.

St. Thomas Assembly Plant

September 12, 1968. For the first time ever, the board of directors of the Ford Motor Company holds its meeting in Canada.

September 1968. The Meteor is twenty years old. It will carry special trim and ornamentation in recognition of its anniversary.

~~~~~

October 11, 1968. Winnipeggers will be flooded no more as the $63 million Red River Floodway opens.

~~~~~

October 16, 1968. Réné Lévesque is chosen to head the Parti Québecois, dedicated to independence and nationhood for Quebec.

~~~~~

December 10, 1968. Ford of Canada breaks an industry record. The highest number of cars produced to date was 419,723 units. Workers in Oakville make history as the 419,724th automobile is built. It is a 1969 Meteor Montcalm convertible, a Canada-only product. This year the Canadian industry tops the 1,000,000 mark for the first time as 1,177,607 cars and trucks are assembled. More than half of the output is exported.

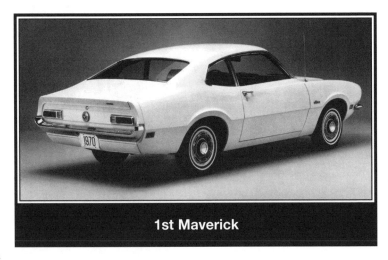

1st Maverick

February 11, 1969. Students lock themselves into the theology department at the University of Windsor to protest university policy. The sit-in will last nine days. Students at Concordia University in Montreal trash the computer centre and set fire to the Hall Building. Police arrest 96 protesters.

Cortina

February 13, 1969. The Montreal Stock Exchange is bombed. Damage is estimated at $1 million.

~ ~ ~ ~ ~

March 11, 1969. It's Skidoos for the RCMP as the last of the sled dogs are retired from active service.

~ ~ ~ ~ ~

March 17, 1969. The first Maverick is built in the St. Thomas, Ontario plant. The public will get to see it on April 17.

Apr il 8, 1969. The Montreal Expos play ball for the very first time, beating the Mets at Shea Stadium. Six days later, the Expos will play their first home game in front of 29,184 fans at Jarry Park and beat the Cards 8 to 7.

~~~~~

April 28, 1969. Folks in the Yukon are glad that Whitehorse Motors Limited is open for business.

~~~~~

May 1969. Maverick is hugely popular with Canadians. A second shift of 1,200 has been added to the St. Thomas plant.

~~~~~

June 23, 1969. Workers in Oakville build the 4-millionth passenger car.

~~~~~

July 20, 1969. More than 30,000 Torontonians gather in Nathan Phillips Square in front of a large-screen television and watch American astronauts walk on the moon's surface.

~~~~~

December 18, 1969. The 500,000th Ford truck is produced.

~~~~~

January 1970. The newly restyled Cortina is unveiled in showrooms. Rising inflation makes it highly popular with thrifty Canadians.

~~~~~

January 1, 1970. Carol Automobile Limitée is the nation's newest Ford dealer, serving residents of Labrador City.

January 26, 1970. Residents in Port Hardy, British Columbia can now buy their Fords and have them serviced at Dave Landon Motors Limited.

~ ~ ~ ~ ~

February 3, 1970. The oil tanker *Arrow* runs aground off the coast of Cape Breton Island. It will break in half, sink and dump nearly 16 million litres of bunker oil into the ocean.

~ ~ ~ ~ ~

April 15, 1970. Six new Cortinas are displayed at the British Auto Show in Montreal. Officials won't know what colours they are until the very last minute because workers in Dagenham are on strike.

~ ~ ~ ~ ~

July 1970. Ford and the UAW begin negotiations. When concluded, the minimum wage will increase from $3.36 an hour to $4.25 1/2 an hour. Thirty-year employees can retire at 58 years of age. Now, a holiday period is paid from before Christmas to New Year's Day.

~ ~ ~ ~ ~

October 5, 1970. British Trade Commissioner, James Cross, is abducted in Montreal. The FLQ claims responsibility and demands $500,000 and the release of political prisoners in exchange for his life. He will be held in captivity for sixty days.

~ ~ ~ ~ ~

October 10, 1970. Labour Minister Pierre Laporte is kidnapped from in front of his home while playing football with his nephew. His body will be found in the trunk of a Chevrolet eight days later.

October 15, 1970. Historians will call it The October Crisis. Citizens are astonished and emotional as soldiers march into Montreal and Quebec City to stop the wave of bombings and kidnappings and to restore law and order.

Roy F. Bennett

November 16, 1970. Roy F. Bennett is elected president of the company. The Winnipeg native is the latest Canadian-born president. A Canadian has been president of the company since Edsel Ford stepped down in 1929."

~~~~~

March 4, 1971. Prime Minister Pierre Elliot Trudeau and Margaret Sinclair exchange wedding vows in Vancouver.

A pril 13, 1971. As of today, Saint Johnners can drop into the showrooms of Parkway Ford-Lincoln in the Loyalist City.

~~~~~

N ovember 1, 1971. The Husky Tower opens in Calgary. It will later be renamed the Calgary Tower. The Olympic Torch used in the 1988 Calgary Olympics will be designed to resemble the landmark.

~~~~~

D ecember 19, 1971. Workers at Ford in the US and Canada now make equal wages.

Ford Pinto Wagon

M arch 1972. The Pinto family grows as a station wagon is introduced.

March 1972. The Mercury Capri gets a V-6. Maverick and Comet get luxury décor packages, too.

~~~~~

April 7, 1972. President Roy Bennett reports that hydrocarbon emissions on Canadian Ford products have been cut by 83 percent. Ford has spent $9,735,000 on pollution control in plants since 1965.

~~~~~

April 15, 1972. U.S. President Nixon is in Ottawa to sign a bilateral pact that will clean up the Great Lakes. No longer will people have to drive around with bumper stickers that read "Lake Erie died for your sins."

~~~~~

May 20, 1972. Humber Motors Limited proudly opens its doors in Corner Brook, Newfoundland.

~~~~~

July 21, 1972. And then there were three. The CRTC grants a license to Global Communications Limited to begin television broadcasting.

~~~~~

September 1972. Meteor turns 25 years old in 1973 and a special, limited edition, Silver Anniversary model marks the occasion. Close to 600,000 Meteors have been built since the 1949 model year.

Meteor's 25th Anniversary

September 1972. Ford is a major TV sponsor of the Canada-Russia world hockey series, which Team Canada wins on the 28th. President Roy Bennett takes to the airwaves to tell Canadians that "We Listen Better." More than 48,000 people will write to Oakville as a result of the advertising campaign. It pays off, Canadians buy more Ford products than ever before in the company's entire 68-year history.

November 9, 1972. *Anik 1* is launched. The latest generation of satellite permits communications anywhere across the country in just seconds.

~~~~~

September 1973. The model year ended with 770 dealers delivering 226,200 cars and 105,300 trucks. This is the last year for the Cortina.

~~~~~

October 17, 1973. Prices for crude oil skyrocket by 70 percent around the world as the Organization of Petroleum Exporting Countries (OPEC) punishes the United States for backing Israel in the recent Yom Kippur War.

Granada

February 1, 1974. Residents of the Queen City can buy cars at Bennett-Dunlop Ford in Regina, Saskatchewan.

~~~~~

February 1974. The newly redesigned Econoline vans are introduced.

~~~~~

July 30, 1974. Bill 22 passes in the National Assembly, making French the only official language in Quebec.

~~~~~

September 17, 1974. The first women are sworn in as RCMP officers. They will earn the same $10,794 a year salary as their male counterparts.

~~~~~

October 1, 1974. Today, 17,186 Ford employees have something to smile about because they are now covered by dental benefits.

~~~~~

October 1974. Dealers shatter model year sales records with deliveries of 225,800 cars and 82,700 trucks on top of that.

~~~~~

November 15, 1974. Inuit leaders of northern Quebec sign the James Bay Agreement with Ottawa and Quebec City. The treaty gives them home rule in a vast, treeless territory that is nearly the size of the State of Texas. The deal takes effect on November 11, 1975.

December 31, 1974. The "precision sized" Ford Granada and Mercury Monarch are smash hits. The country's 745 dealers are delighted. Records show that the pair has sold 6,278 units compared to a total of 4,344 units sold by four domestic competitors. A full 40 percent of trade-ins for Granada and Monarch are competitors' compacts.

~~~~~

January 1, 1975. It is the United Nations International Women's Year. Ford of Canada will bestow eight university scholarships upon women in order to study for their master's of business administration.

~~~~~

March 1975. The newly updated Mercury Bobcat is introduced. Formerly a Canada-only model, Bobcat will now be offered to Americans, too.

Bobcat

March 4, 1975. Action! The House of Commons is equipped with TV cameras. We get to watch as Grits thump their desks and Tories applaud their leaders' remarks.

~~~~~

April 4, 1975. There are 2,500,000 Ford owners across Canada.

~~~~~

April 26, 1975. Stockholders approve of the name *Ford du Canada, Limitée* as the company's legal name in French.

~~~~~

June 27, 1975. L'Anse aux Meadows National Park is dedicated by PM Trudeau. The 8,000-hectare park was home to the first Viking settlement in the New World. Now the archaeological site will be protected. It will become a United Nations World Heritage Site in 1978.

~~~~~

July 30, 1975. Petro-Canada comes into existence by Parliamentary decree to protect national interest in the oil industry. The retail chain stretches from coast to coast, made up from the purchase of Petrofina in the eastern provinces and Pacific 66 in the west.

~~~~~

September 1975. The new Ford, Mercury and Lincolns are introduced. There are sixteen models offered to Canadians that are not available in the US market. They include the Bobcat Special, Pinto Special, Cougar S, Ford Custom 500 and Mercury Marquis Monarch. These Canada-only cars account for 20 percent of the 756 Ford and Mercury dealers' sales.

October 4, 1975. Mirabel Airport opens to great fanfare. The glitzy $55 million facility located midway between Montreal and Ottawa will never take off and be mothballed by the end of the century.

F-Series

October 1, 1975. Avenue Ford is ready for business. The dealership will serve many of Montreal's West Islanders from its Sources Boulevard home in Dollard-des-Ormeaux.

~ ~ ~ ~ ~

December 1975. Olympic fever sweeps the nation. Production of the red-and-white Ford Olympic Pintos and Mercury Olympic Bobcats begin. Each car will carry the official emblem of the Canadian Olympic Association and a portion of each sale will be donated to Canadian athletes.

Dec, 1975. Ottawa cracks down on runaway inflation with the establishment of the Anti-Inflation Board. The federal agency has final word on establishing fair prices and wages, though few will like it.

~~~~~

December 31, 1975. It is the last day for residents of Ontario to buy a new car without paying sales tax.

~~~~~

December 31, 1975. Ford is Number One in trucks. One out of every three trucks sold in Canada wears a blue oval whether it is the little Courier, an F-series or the massive WT-9000.

~~~~~

January 1, 1976. Say goodbye to miles, Imperial gallons and pounds-per-square inch. Canada is officially metric. Speed and distance are now measured in kilometres, gasoline is pumped by the litre and air pressure is measured in kilopasquales per square metre. Road signs won't change until September of 1977.

~~~~~

March 18, 1976. Settled by Icelandic immigrants in the 1870s, the good folk of Gimli, Manitoba can now buy Fords at Gimli Auto Limited.

~~~~~

April 2, 1976. Roy Bennett, president of Ford of Canada, tells stockholders that 75 percent of the company's production is being exported to the United States.

10-Millionth Canadian Ford

April 1976. The Canada-only Special Edition Granada and Special Edition Monarch are introduced. These lesser-priced cars will boost sales significantly, pushing Ford's percentage of the compact market to 27.5 percent up from 26.7 percent in 1974.

~~~~~

June 26, 1976. The CN Tower opens in Toronto. It is the world's tallest free-standing structure.

~~~~~

July 14, 1976. Members of Parliament vote to abolish capital punishment. There will be no more public hangings of criminals.

July 17, 1976. Queen Elizabeth II officially opens the 21st Summer Olympics in Montreal. The Olympic Stadium is not yet complete despite its $1 billion price tag. We become the first host country in Olympic history not to win gold.

~ ~ ~ ~ ~

August 9, 1976. There is no place too remote for people to own and operate Fords. Kingland Ford opens in Hay River, NWT to take care of citizens' Ford needs.

~ ~ ~ ~ ~

August 19, 1976. The 10-millionth Canadian Ford is built, exactly 72 years and two days after the company was founded in 1904. The honour falls to a Ford Pinto as it rolls out the doors of the St. Thomas assembly plant.

~ ~ ~ ~ ~

September 1976. Ford owners whose 1970 to 1974 cars have prematurely rusted can apply for a $300 certificate to trade in their cars for new models, now protected against rust by the Duragard System.

~ ~ ~ ~ ~

November 1976. A long strike is settled but the loss of production in Ford's Canadian plants is estimated at 53,000 cars.

~ ~ ~ ~ ~

November 15, 1976. Réné Lévésque and the Parti Québecois will form the next majority government in Quebec City.

Novermber 1976. Ford offers an optional warranty good for 36 months or 36,000 miles. The offer is good on cars up to three years old and costs from $90 on Bobcats and Pintos to $195 on Lincolns.

~~~~~

December 31, 1976. There are 765 Ford and Mercury dealers across the nation.

Lincoln Mk I, II and III

February 28, 1977. ViaRail is established. The new Crown corporation will amalgamate the money losing passenger train services of the CNR and CP Rail.

~~~~~

April 7, 1977. The Toronto Blue Jays play their first home game. Of course, it snows to beat the band but the Jays whip the White Sox 11 to 5, despite the white stuff.

August 7, 1977. Ford is a proud sponsor of the Canada Summer Games in St. John's, Newfoundland.

~~~~~

August 26, 1977. Throughout Quebec, the Charter of the French Language becomes law.

~~~~~

September 1977. Ford extends the warranty on all new 1978 cars to 12 months or 20,000 kilometres. This reflects the new law making Canada metric.

~~~~~

December 31, 1977. There are 761 Ford and Mercury-Lincoln dealers across the country.

~~~~~

January 30, 1978. Canadians learn that soldiers have found the impact crater from a Soviet spy satellite that crashed in the Northwest Territories.

~~~~~

April 5, 1978. The company kicks off its Diamond Jubilee. President Roy Bennett poses with a 1904 Model C and a brand new Mercury Marquis. The Model C will be placed on exhibit at Ontario Place where half a million visitors will see it. Exactly 340 pre-1959 cars will make it to Oakville for the Ford Homecoming. At the end of the model year, the company will have sold 846,000 passenger cars here and abroad.

June 3, 1978. Founded by the kite-flying Benjamin Franklin, *The Gazette*, celebrates its 200th birthday. Montreal's morning newspaper is the oldest continuously published newspaper in the country.

~~~~~

June 19, 1978. Ovale Ford opens for business on St. Jacques Street in Montreal.

~~~~~

May 22, 1979. Joe Clark and his Tories win the election. The new government will fall in nine months, victim of a non-confidence motion in the House.

~~~~~

August 1979. Sales of Ford products hit a record $7.1 billion. Despite the phenomenal figure, the company will end the year in the hole by $12 million, the first red ink seen by stockholders since 1946.

~~~~~

August 18, 1979. The Dempster Highway opens. The surfaced road is 645 kilometres in length and runs from Dawson City to Inuvik.

~~~~~

October 23, 1979. *The Globe & Mail* becomes "Canada's National Newspaper." Not just for Torontonians anymore, satellite signals feed local presses across the nation and readers buy the paper locally.

~~~~~

October 27, 1979. Premier René Lévésque turns on the power and hydro-electricity flows from the $15 billion James Bay facility into the provincial energy grid.

December 31, 1979. Six children of employees are attending university on scholarships awarded by Ford of Canada. Since 1954, a total of 145 scholarships have been given to children of employees.

~~~~~

March 13, 1980. Dealers have sold 339,000 vehicles in 1979, up 1 percent from 1978.

Ford Escort

April 12, 1980. Terry Fox begins his cross-country run in St. John's. The 22-year old has already lost one leg to cancer. His Marathon of Hope will raise money for cancer research. He will get as far as Thunder Bay and raise $2 million before finding out that cancer has spread to his lungs.

Apri1 22, 1980. Officials report that Canadians have purchased $1 billion worth of Ford vehicles from 771 Ford and Lincoln Mercury dealers.

~~~~~

May 10, 1980. Ottawa gives Chrysler Canada a $200 million loan guarantee to keep the troubled auto maker in business. Officials at Studebaker Canada would have appreciated that gesture in March of 1964.

~~~~~

May 22, 1980. Quebecers vote in a referendum to remain in Confederation.

1981 Mercury Lynx

June 27, 1980. By act of Parliament, *O Canada* becomes the national anthem. *God Save the Queen* is now the royal anthem.

~ ~ ~ ~ ~

July 1980. The new aluminum plant comes on line in Windsor. It makes cylinder heads and intake manifolds.

~ ~ ~ ~ ~

October 1980. Dealers introduce the new Escort and Lynx. By year's end, 6,000 units will have been delivered, twice as many as the models it replaced.

~ ~ ~ ~ ~

December 31, 1980. The economic downturn has caused a shakeout as dealers drop from 771 to 754. There are still 13,395 workers on payroll but 5,112 have been laid off until the business climate improves.

~ ~ ~ ~ ~

January 1, 1981. Business is down in the dumps right across the country. The dollar has plunged from $US1.06 to a low of 85 cents in the last twelve months.

~ ~ ~ ~ ~

February 16, 1981. Production of the Ford EXP and the Mercury LN7, begins as sport coupes roll off the lines in St. Thomas. They hold the distinction of being the first front-wheel drive automobiles to be built in the country.

~ ~ ~ ~ ~

March 30, 1981. President Roy Bennett writes that total 1980 sales were off by 36 percent, down to 239,800 units.

May 1981. The engine plant begins production of a new, fuel efficient V-6 engine.

~~~~~

June 28, 1981. Terry Fox dies of cancer in a New Westminister, British Columbia hospital at sunrise. The Prime Minister orders all flags across the country to be flown at half-mast until his funeral. Millions pay tribute to the young man's courage each fall as they participate in the annual Terry Fox Run.

Ken Harrigan and the Ford Team

November 14, 1981. It's success in outer space for the Remote Manipulator System, better known as Canadarm. Designed and built by Spar Aerospace of Toronto, the arm moves satellites and other cargo in and out of the space shuttle Columbia's bay.

November 21, 1981. More than 100,000 angry demonstrators gather on Parliament Hill to protest high interest rates that have hit 15 percent. It is the largest demonstration in national history.

~~~~~

January 1, 1982. Roy F. Bennett is now chairman of the board. After ten years behind the president's desk, the Winnipeg native is replaced by Kenneth Harrigan. Calendar year sales of passenger cars is 136,560 units and 86,759 trucks.

~~~~~

February 15, 1982.   A violent storm causes the oil rig *Ocean Ranger* to collapse off the coast of Newfoundland and sink into the Atlantic. The final count is 84 lives lost.

~~~~~

March 1982. Ford and GM ask to negotiate with the Canadian United Auto Workers Union. Bob White, Director says they must wait for mid-summer talks. He will negotiate a Cost of Living Allowance based on a Canadian price index, not on the previous US-influenced bilateral formula.

Tempo and Topaz Roll Out

March 30, 1982. President Kenneth Harrigan reports that quality is up 25 percent over last year and that 27.4 percent of all small specialty cars sold in Canada are Ford products. He notes that the addition of a station wagon to the Escort and Lynx mix has pushed their sales up to 11 percent of the market.

~~~~~

April 17, 1982. More than 30,000 gather on Parliament Hill to watch Queen Elizabeth sign the Constitution and deliver it to Prime Minister Trudeau. Canada has cut its last legal apron strings to the United Kingdom.

~~~~~

April 28, 1982. Stockholders learn that Ford has lost $214 million. President Bennett identifies the weak Canadian dollar and the incredible rise of the Japanese in the domestic market as the reasons for the downturn.

~~~~~

March 1983. The first 1984 Ford Tempo is built in Oakville. Now the Canadian company's passenger car production is all front-wheel drive.

~~~~~

March 30, 1983. Officials are pleased to report that quality has improved by 40 percent over the 1980 models and that Ford sold 112,600 cars during the 1982 model season. Although the sales are off by 18.1 percent, the domestic industry as a whole fared worse with a drop of 21.2 percent.

~~~~~

April 26, 1983. Ford stockholders learn that 48.6 percent of all automobiles purchased by Canadians are in the small car segment.

May 1983. Tempo and Topaz roll out the doors of the Oakville Assembly Plant. The company spent $115 million to retool and modernize the plant for the new cars.

~ ~ ~ ~ ~

May 1983. The economy is still performing poorly. There are 632 Ford and Lincoln-Mercury dealers and another 115 tractor dealerships across the country.

~ ~ ~ ~ ~

June 19, 1983. BC Place opens in Vancouver. The domed stadium seats 60,000 spectators.

~ ~ ~ ~ ~

November 1983. A new $55 million assembly flexibility programme in the St. Thomas plant allows full-sized Ford Crown Victorias and Mercury Grand Marquis to be built on the same line as the subcompact Ford Escorts and Mercury Lynx. The mix is 45 full-sized cars and five subcompacts per hour.

~ ~ ~ ~ ~

December 23, 1983. Jeanne Sauvé is named Governor-General. The Saskatchewan native is an experienced broadcaster and a veteran politician. She is also the first woman to be head of state.

~ ~ ~ ~ ~

January 1, 1984. The year starts with 650 Ford and Lincoln-Mercury dealers and 130 Ford tractor dealerships spread out across the land.

February 29, 1984. After his famous 'long walk in the snow,' Pierre Trudeau announces that sixteen years as prime minister is long enough. He will step down as PM and retire from politics altogether.

1985 Crown Victoria

March 1984. The pay cheque grows larger for Ford employees as a 28-cent an hour pay rise goes into effect.

~~~~~

March 30, 1984. After four years of red ink, Ford recovers. Employment is back to 16,100, where it was in 1979. Sales for the 1983 model year rose to 128,000 units.

~~~~~

September 4, 1984. Brian Mulroney and his Tories win a massive landslide in the federal election, taking all but 71 seats in the House of Commons.

September 9, 1984. Pope John Paul II becomes the first reigning pontiff to visit Canada. He will tour the country for eleven days. His Holiness will fill Olympic Stadium in Montreal to its 84,000-seat capacity as well as the 60,000-seat BC Place in Vancouver.

~~~~~

October 5, 1984. Marc Garneau becomes the first Canadian astronaut to see the world from outer space.

~~~~~

October 1984. The Canadian United Auto Workers and Ford sign a three-year deal without a strike.

~~~~~

February 1985. The St. Thomas, Ontario plant is the world's sole source for Marquis and Crown Vics now that the St. Louis, Missouri plant has switched over to building Aerostars.

~~~~~

March 29, 1985. Sales for the just closed 1984 model year showed an increase of 27 percent in the passenger car market as 128,034 units were sold. Truck sales rose by 32 percent with 90,131 units delivered.

~~~~~

March 7, 1985. The board of directors votes a dividend of $14 a share.

1985 Merkur XR4Ti

May 1985. The Merkur XR4Ti is introduced to Canadians. 749 of the exotic Euro-Merks will be sold by year's end.

~~~~~

June 20, 1985. René Lévésque, Premier of Quebec, announces his intention to retire from politics.

~~~~~

June 23, 1985. An Air India jet explodes off the coast of Ireland. Most the passengers on board the Boeing 747 are Canadian. All 329 lives are lost.

~~~~~

December 1985. Ford's Tempo has a sales upswing to 47,692 units across the country but it is eclipsed by the upstart Hyundai Pony. The Korean import is Canada's best selling automobile with 56,000 sales. Needless to say, the domestic automakers are not pleased and demand that Ottawa rethink South Korea's duty-free status as a "developing nation."

Decmber 12, 1985. A chartered jet crashes near Gander, Newfoundland. All 285 on board are killed. Many of the dead are American soldiers.

~ ~ ~ ~ ~

January 1, 1986. Ford starts the new year with 676 car and 141 tractor dealers in place to serve the nation. The company has 29,700 employees on staff to build and keep those vehicles on the road.

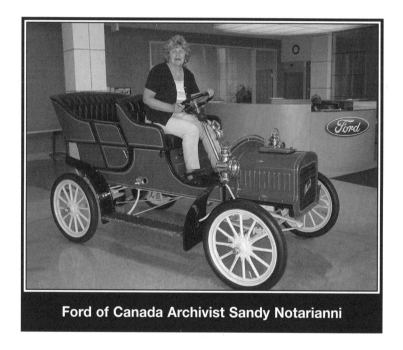

Ford of Canada Archivist Sandy Notarianni

April 1986. Sandy Notarianni joins Herm Smith in the Archives and Historical Department.

May 2, 1986. Prince Charles and Princess Diana open the World's Fair in Vancouver. Expo 86 will receive 22 million visitors during its year-long run.

~~~~~

May 8, 1986. Ottawa advises citizens not to drink rainwater because it contains high levels of radioactive iodine, believed to have swept the country after the nuclear disaster in Chernobyl.

~~~~~

May 13, 1986. All of Ford's products now carry a new four-year/80,000-kilometre warranty on the power train and the five-year Duragard anti-corrosion and perforation warranty on the body.

~~~~~

August 1986. Statistics show that the most popular new vehicle in Alberta, Saskatchewan and Manitoba is Ford's F-150 pickup. Prince Edward Islanders like Ford too, but want to keep things in smaller perspective. Islanders buy more Ford Rangers than any other new vehicle. British Columbians prefer the Honda Accord. New Brunswickers and Nova Scotians' favourite new car is the Dodge Aries. Newfoundlanders and Quebecers have purchased more Chevrolet Cavaliers than any other nameplate In Ontario, the Pontiac 6000 takes top honours.

~~~~~

October 1986. The new Mercury Tracer, imported from Ford's Taiwanese subsidiary racks up 1,329 sales by year's end. It replaces the Lynx in the stable.

November 18, 1986. MPPs at Queen's Park vote unanimously to provide services for Ontarians in French as well as English.

~~~~~

January 16, 1987. Naber Ford Sales hangs up its shingle in Shellbrook, Saskatchewan.

~~~~~

March 3, 1987. Ford stockholders will receive a dividend of $6 a share.

~~~~~

April 16, 1987. President Harrigan reports that 1986 was Ford's best year since 1979. Sales of 188,800 cars and 124,626 trucks were the magic numbers that made it happen. Ford is Number One in the truck game.

~~~~~

May 22, 1987. Rick Hansen arrives home in Vancouver after a gruelling 40,000-kilometre, 34-nation trek around the world in his wheelchair. During his travels, the now paraplegic, one-time athlete visited Oakville where Ford and its employees both contributed generously to the cause. The hero has raised more than $10 million for spinal cord injury research.

~~~~~

June 3, 1987. Exhausted first ministers have bargained in a 19-hour marathon session. They put their signatures on the Meech Lake Accord. When ratified in each province, Quebec will be a full partner in Confederation. It will not happen.

July 1987. Ford and General Motors jointly file dumping charges against Hyundai Auto Canada Inc. Revenue Canada finds Hyundai guilty in December and adds a special 6 percent duty on its imported products.

~~~~~

August 1987. Ford products are the number one selling vehicles in Alberta, Manitoba, New Brunswick, Nova Scotia, Quebec and Saskatchewan.

~~~~~

August 30, 1987. Ben Johnson wins the 100-metre dash in Rome in 9.83 seconds, breaking the world record. He will win gold at the Olympics in Seoul but be stripped of his medal when he tests positive for steroids.

~~~~~

October 29, 1987. Baie Comeau, Quebec, gets a new Ford dealer when Lafléche Auto (1987) Limitée hangs its sign on boulevard Lafléche.

F250 XLT Lariat SuperCab

December 11, 1987. Opposition leaders are angry as Prime Minister Brian Mulroney tables a bill proposing free trade with the United States in the House of Commons.

~~~~~

December 31, 1987. Ford's F-series is the best selling vehicle in the country for the second year in a row. Tempo is the best selling passenger car with 42,320 units finding homes in garages across the nation. Car sales hit 188,862 units for the 1986 model year.

~~~~~

January 1, 1988. The company starts the year with 681 dealers who will sell 207,539 cars and 148,336 trucks during the 1988 model year.

~~~~~

February 13, 1988. The 15th Winter Olympics open in Calgary. Canadian athletes will not win any gold medals.

~~~~~

March 22, 1988. The gut-wrenching movie, *Un Zoo la nuit* (Night Zoo) wins 13 Genies.

~~~~~

August 17, 1988. The Ford Motor Company of Canada, Limited marks its 85th year in business.

~~~~~

December 31, 1988. Ford's tractor and Equipment Operations were sold to New Holland of Canada Limited during the year. The company will concentrate on cars and trucks.

Decmber 31, 1988. Shareholders are delighted to watch their profit line triple to $270 million. Most of the increase comes from the sale of the subsidiary in the Republic of South Africa. $100 million was spent to upgrade the paint shop in St. Thomas. It now uses the "2K" urethane base coat, clear coat process, heretofore the exclusive domain of Mercedes-Benz.

Ford Tractors and Backhoes

January 1989. The Free Trade Agreement takes effect. Thousands of jobs will disappear as companies move their operations to the United States.

~~~~~

January 1989. Both Ford and Mercury dealers get the micro-sized Festiva. The imported econobox is slotted in the "Basic-Small" segment of the market.

January 20, 1989. Lacombe Ford Sales Limited sets up shop in Lacombe, Alberta.

~ ~ ~ ~ ~

April 7, 1989. A Greyhound bus headed from Montreal to New York City is hijacked and driven to Ottawa where it is parked on Parliament Hill. A gunman threatens to blow it up along with the ten passengers. He eventually surrenders.

1989 Ford Festiva

April 20, 1989. The last $1 bills roll out of the presses at the Canadian Bank Note Company Limited. We will quickly get used to the new $1 coin, better known as the "loony."

June 3, 1989. Toronto's SkyDome is officially opened.

~~~~~

August 11, 1989. The Canadian Automobile Association releases figures showing that it costs more than $100 a week to own and operate even the cheapest car. The CAA's president points fingers at Ottawa for the high cost. The federal government slaps a huge tax on each litre of gasoline bought.

~~~~~

November 30, 1989. The luxurious, fast and imported Merkur is a slow but steady seller, with 755 units sold to date for the calendar year.

~~~~~

December 6, 1989. Fourteen female engineering students, attending a computer class in the Ecole Polytechnique faculty of the University of Montreal, are gunned down in cold blood by Marc Lepine, who then kills himself with his semi-automatic rifle.

~~~~~

December 1, 1989. Jaguar's Board of Directors accept Ford's offer to purchase the company. Britain's House of Commons has already voted in favour of adding an amendment to the company's charter to permit the sale.

~~~~~

December 31, 1989. Ford of Canada outdoes itself, earning $44 million more than it did last year. It's the second best year in the company's 85-year history. The increase came primarily from strong sales in its wholly owned subsidiaries in New Zealand and Australia. Sales across this country were off by $17 million.

January 16, 1990. Avalon Ford in St. John's, Newfoundland is ready to do business with Townies and Baymen, too.

~ ~ ~ ~ ~

September 1990. An eight-day strike is settled and renovations at both the St. Thomas and Oakville plants get under way. St. Thomas gets the Crown Victoria and Grand Marquis that will start rolling out the doors in January of 1991. $200 million is being pumped into the aging Oakville plant. It will be the home of the new mid-sized vans.

~ ~ ~ ~ ~

October 1, 1990. James O'Connor becomes president of the company. Kenneth Harrigan becomes Chairman of the Board and CEO.

~ ~ ~ ~ ~

December 31, 1990. Ford of Canada posts a loss of $57 million. Sales were down at home as consumers waited for the implementation of the new Goods & Services Tax to take place next year. Sales were off in Australia and New Zealand, too. The strike here at home didn't help much. Tempo slips to number three in popularity.

~ ~ ~ ~ ~

January 1, 1991. Finance Minister Michael Wilson has shepherded the unpopular Goods and Services Tax all the way from a Green Paper to Royal Assent. The law takes effect today, though it will be 7 percent not the 9 percent that Wilson wanted. The GST will prompt auto sales to drop by 4 percent and truck sales to tumble 9 percent throughout the industry.

~ ~ ~ ~ ~

January 1991. The last three Merkurs are sold and there will be no more of the posh German import.

May 14, 1991. Stockholders learn that the company has spent nearly $1 billion to upgrade the Oakville, St. Thomas and Windsor plants with the latest state-of-the-art manufacturing technology.

~~~~~

July 1991. Herm Smith dies. In 1968, he founded the company archives and served as the company historian for nearly a quarter of a century. The fact that you are able to enjoy this book today is because he passionately cared about preserving Ford—and Canada's legacy.

Herm Smith and Model C

December 31, 1991. The top ten selling cars in Canada this year are Chevrolet Cavalier, Honda Civic, Honda Accord, Pontiac Sunbird, Ford Tempo, Toyota Tercel, Mercury Topaz, Toyota Corolla, Ford Taurus and Ford Escort. Ford of Canada Limited declares a net loss of $85 million for the year as compared to a $10.1 million profit in 1990.

May 19, 1992. Despite $4.4 billion worth of sales, the company lost $209 million. Unfair import rules are the cause of so much red ink.

Hydrogen Fuel Cell Engine

July 1, 1992. Canada is 125 years old. CEO Kenneth Harrigan says proudly, "I choose…a revitalized and vibrant Canada. I choose a Canada in which there are distinct societies, all of them national treasures."

~~~~~

December 31, 1992. Unemployment stands at 11.3 percent and the dollar has dropped to 82.7 cents in US currency.

~~~~~

March 1993. The Premier Automotive Group is formed by Ford. Ultimately it will include Jaguar, Volvo, Land Rover and Aston-Martin.

1993 Taurus LX Wagon

May 18, 1993. Ford is environmentally conscious. It is reported that the Essex Engine plant recycles more than 300,000 litres of waste industrial oil annually The Niagara Glass Plant recycles 7,700 tons of glass a year. The Central Office in Oakville recycles enough paper to equal thirty-five trees every week.

~~~~~

June 10, 1993. As of today, Clarenville Ford Sales Limited in Newfoundland will take good care of folks around Trinity Bay.

~~~~~

August 1993. Sales for the 1992 model year were 259,469 units delivered, up 5.5 percent from the previous year. It's the best year for the company since 1989. Ford owns 22.8 percent of the domestic market.

October 8, 1993. Thompson Ford Sales Ltd. hangs out its shingle in Thompson, Manitoba.

~~~~~

October 1993. The Tories are swept from power in the most stunning electoral upset in history. In fact, with only two seats the Progressive Conservatives are no longer an officially recognized political party. Pundits joke that Jean Charest and Elsie Wayne, the entire Tory caucus, can meet in a phone booth.

~~~~~

December 31, 1993. The top ten selling cars for the year are the Chevrolet Cavalier, Honda Civic, Pontiac Sunbird, Ford Taurus, Ford Tempo, Mercury Topaz, Honda Accord, Pontiac Grand AM, Toyota Camry and Toyota Tercel.

~~~~~

April 1994. Hertz becomes a wholly owned subsidiary of Ford.

1996 Ford Ranger XLT SuperCab

July 1994. Ford purchases the outstanding 25 percent of Aston-Martin Lagonda Limited.

~~~~~

October 1994. The 1994 model year ends with sales of 282,000 Ford vehicles, up 10 percent from 1993.

~~~~~

December 31, 1994. The Gross Domestic Product grew by 4.5 percent during the past twelve months.

~~~~~

January 1, 1995. Ford starts the year with a little well-deserved bubbly as its F-Series truck is the number one selling truck for 29 years in a row. The dollar is worth only 71 cents in US currency.

~~~~~

March 1995. A week-long rail strike prevents any Fords from rolling out of the factory doors.

~~~~~

February 1996. Our pockets grow heavier as the $2 coin is introduced. Better known as the "toonie," the coin is made of nickel with a bronze centre. Featuring Queen Elizabeth on the face and two polar bears on the back side, the coin will last 20 times longer than the red $2 bill it replaces.

~~~~~

July 11, 1996. Folks in Alma, Quebec can have their Fords serviced at the dealership as the Alma Ford Inc. sign goes up in town.

June 24, 1997. It is 500 years ago today that John Cabot disembarked from the *Matthew* in Bonavista to claim this "New Founde Land" for Britain.

2000 Ford Focus

October 3, 1997. For the 1996 model year, Ford has sold 299,289 cars, up 11.9 percent from 1995. Truck sales rose 22.1 percent at 188,479 units sold.

~ ~ ~ ~ ~

March 12, 1998. Peace River Ford Sales, Inc. is ready for business on 100th Avenue NE in Peace River, Alberta.

~ ~ ~ ~ ~

September 2, 1998. A SwissAir jet crashes off the coast of Nova Scotia killing all 229 people on board.

October 1998. Lincoln sales across Canada totaled 4,372 units and 25,181 Mercurys were delivered during the 1997 model year.

~~~~~

January 5, 1999. The company can brag that in its 94-year history, the 1998 selling season was the second best ever for trucks as 176,936 haulers were delivered.

~~~~~

March 31, 1999. Ford purchases Volvo's passenger car division. The Swedish automaker's assembly plant in Halifax will close at the end of the year.

~~~~~

October 1, 1999. The Ford Focus is launched. Canadians take home 2,179 of the "Expect More" cars in its first month on the market.

~~~~~

January 6, 2000. The 1,500,000th Ford engine is built in Windsor.

~~~~~

January 26, 2000. Ford of Canada posts 1999 consolidated sales revenues of $30 billion, an increase of 13 percent compared to 1998. Bobbie Gaunt, President and CEO reports that the company has 14,000 employees and 568 dealers. Ford of Canada's domestic vehicle sales of 282,453 units were up 4 percent compared to 271,479 in 1998. The company's three Canadian vehicle assembly plants built an all-time record 685,517 cars and trucks in 1999, surpassing the previous year's production by 9.6 percent. The Ontario Truck Plant produced 114,676 F-Series pickups in 1999, a 2.3 percent increase. The F-Series was Canada's best-selling truck for the 34th year and the top-selling vehicle in Canada for the sixth consecutive year.

February 17, 2000. Members of the Automobile Journalists Association of Canada (AJAC) vote for the Ford Focus as Car of the Year.

2001 Lincoln Navigator

March 15, 2000. Hydro-Quebec orders a Ford Ranger Electric Vehicle. It is the first Canadian company to do so.

~~~~~

May 2000. Ford acquires Land Rover from BMW for USD $2.7 billion.

~~~~~

May 2, 2000. Officials announce that Ford of Canada is the new sponsor of the Francofolies Festival in Montreal.

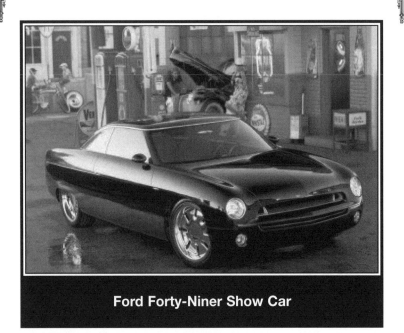

Ford Forty-Niner Show Car

May 26, 2000. The Ford Motor Company of Canada, Limited will sponsor a Children's Safety Village to teach children how to protect themselves in case of fire or other danger. The village will be built in the Fanshawe Conservation Area near London, Ontario.

~~~~~

June 2000. The company has five manufacturing plants and three vehicle assembly plants in Canada. Some 17,000 people work directly for Ford of Canada and another 22,400 work for the 565 dealers across the country.

~~~~~

December 19, 2000. Moncton Ford-Lincoln Sales Limited hangs out its shingle for folks in this New Brunswick city.

November 12, 2001. Percival Ford-Lincoln opens its doors in Regina, Saskatchewan.

~~~~~

September 7, 2002. The CBC and Radio-Canada celebrate a half-century of public television broadcasting with a 50th Anniversary train that leaves Vancouver and will travel across the country.

~~~~~

September 13, 2002. Ford's Living Legends Tour arrives in Toronto. The show includes the GT40 super concept car, both versions of the Ford Forty-Niner and two special, limited edition production Mustangs – the Mach 1 and the Pony.

Centennial Edition Vehicles

October 9, 2002. Queen Elizabeth II visits Toronto during her 50th year on the throne. She will see the new Ford Windstar and learn that it is all-Canadian. Ford's employees are featured in a special video to mark Her Majesty's half century as the reigning monarch.

~ ~ ~ ~ ~

November 11, 2002. The 17th Annual Gemini Awards are hosted by comic Sean Cullen. *DaVinci's Inquest* takes home a Gemini for best drama, best comedy is *An American in Canada*. Colm Feore receives a well-deserved Gemini as best actor for his portrayal of the country's fifteenth Prime Minister in the mini-series *Trudeau*.

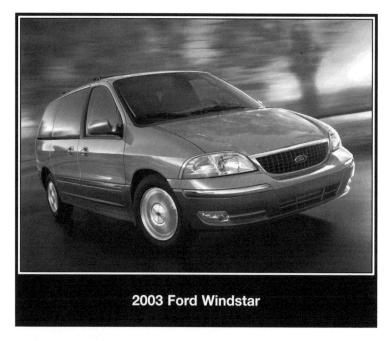

2003 Ford Windstar

January 3, 2003. Folks across the country bought 258,807 Ford and Lincoln vehicles in the 2002 calendar year. The sales total was up 2.8 percent over 2001. The F-Series trucks are the nation's favourite for the thirty-seventh year in a row!

February 13, 2003. The Toronto International Auto Show opens. On display in the Ford exhibit are five specially trimmed Centennial vehicles including a limited edition Taurus, Focus, Mustang, Explorer and an F-Series Super Duty Crew Cab. Only 3,000 of the Centennial passenger cars and 4,000 of the trucks will be produced.

3V Triton 5.4L V-8 Engine

March 27, 2003. The dollar rises to 68.3 cents in US currency.

~~~~~

April 13, 2003. For years, people asked the riddle, "What's the difference between Hell and Quebec?" The answer was, "In Hell, you can turn right on red." As of today, Quebecers can legally turn right on a red light for the first time—except on the Island of Montreal.

April 16, 2003. The Global Village grows. Ford sales in Canada, the United States and Mexico are now reported together as one unit. On a pre-tax basis, Ford's automotive sector earned $659 million during the first quarter of 2003, a much brighter picture than the loss of $370 million recorded this time a year ago.

2003 GT-40

April 28, 2003. Ford of Canada employs 16,000 people and has 502 dealers across the country.

~~~~~

April 29, 2003. Workers in Windsor complete the corporation's 100-millionth V-8 engine. The milestone mill is a 3V Triton, 5.4-litre power plant, slated for an F-150 truck. The first V-8 engine was rolled off the lines in Windsor seventy-nine years ago. Nearly one out of every four of the V-8 engines built worldwide by Ford has come from the Windsor plant.

April 30, 2003. More than a thousand people in British Columbia, Ontario, Quebec and New Brunswick have been quarantined and twenty-three have died of Severe Acute Respiratory Disease. Yesterday, the World Health Organization lifted its travel ban on Toronto, where all of the SARS deaths in this country have occurred.

~~~~~

May 1, 2003. The loony hits a five-year high. It is worth 70.44 cents against the US dollar.

~~~~~

June 16, 2003. The Ford Motor Company, Inc. marks its 100th anniversary worldwide and is the parent of the Ford Motor Company of Canada, Limited.

Testing Ford Focus for Canadian Winters

August 2003. It is the Diamond Jubilee of the International Twin Cities programme. President Roosevelt and Premier Stalin first instituted the idea to promote solidarity among the citizens of Allied nations during World War Two. Halifax is twinned with Hakodate, Japan. Odessa, Ukraine and Vancouver share special ties. In Quebec, the village of St. Elisabeth is twinned with Sanankoroba, Mali and Toronto's sister city is Amsterdam, Holland.

~ ~ ~ ~ ~

August 14, 2003. 4:10 p.m. and 50 million North Americans are in the dark, as an enormous hydro failure affects 12 million Ontarians. Toronto and New York City are particularly chaotic.

~ ~ ~ ~ ~

April 30, 2004. Today is the last day to get those tax forms in the mail. Quebecers fill out a separate form for Revenu Quebec. More than 21 million of us file, half do so on the Internet.

~ ~ ~ ~ ~

July 1, 2004. Canada turns 137 years old today. Citizens celebrate the occasion with picnics, concerts and fireworks.

~ ~ ~ ~ ~

August 17, 2004. Ford marks a century of building automobiles and trucks in Canada and enters its second century as a healthy and vital part of the country's economy.

ACKNOWLEDGEMENTS

First and foremost a very special thanks goes to Sandy Notarianni, Historical Consultant at the Ford Motor Company of Canada, Limited for her tireless efforts to make sure that this book actually saw the light of day.

I wish to thank colleagues, especially Patrick Foster, automotive historian. Without his encouragement, I would never have started writing automotive histories. Jan and Murray MacEwan at *Old Autos* deserve a special thanks for taking a chance on an unknown writer as well as Pat Ertel at *Vintage Truck*, Chad and Katie Elmore at *Belt Pulley* and also Keith Mathiowetzk and Angelo Van Bogart at *Old Cars*.

Then there are my friends and family, the true believers who have stuck with me through thick and thin. Thanks to Diego Argaez, Howard Belsky and Glenn Burt, Mario Charbonneau and Nathalie Maillet, Reid and Margaret Coolen, Alice D'Odean, Neil and Eleanor Gaskin, Lila Gottheil, Lois Graham, Randy Green, Mike Grella, Lee and Michelle Hastings, Dave and Clare Ivany, Jason Ives and Catherine McIntosh, Anne Jared, Paul Lehman, Gerry and Mark Lehman, Myke and Penny Leonard, Elizabeth Miller, Wayne and Becky Mays, Gordon Mays, John and Dot Oakes, John Oakes and Perry Aleski, Dorothy Jean Perkins, the Plenderleiths, Beverly Reeves, Andrès Runnels, Rob Saunders, Carole Shepard, Craig Shoemaker, Dick and Lely Tucker, Olivier Vendette, Robert Vock and Craig Zemeitas.

Finally, a *gros merci* goes to Francois Pigeon who is not only a dear friend and the very best mechanic in the world but occasionally pretends I don't owe him anything for parts or labour, claiming my Rambler is still under warranty!

James Mays
Montreal, Quebec
August 17, 2003